Teacher Was a White Witch

Teacher
Was a White Witch

by Myrliss Hershey

W

THE WESTMINSTER PRESS
Philadelphia

Published by The Westminster Press ®
Philadelphia, Pennsylvania

PRINTED IN THE UNITED STATES OF AMERICA

Library of Congress Cataloging in Publication Data

Hershey, Myrliss, 1928–
    Teacher was a white witch.

    Bibliography: p.
    1. Open plan schools. 2. School integration—United States. 3. Teaching. I. Title.
LB1029.06H47   372.1′3   72-12981
ISBN 0-664-20963-7

Contents

Introduction

The Office of Education issued an ultimatum: the school system had to formulate an integration compliance plan or lose important federal monies. And so the "busing for racial balance" controversy raged. Lists of pros and cons were picked up by the news media and condensed into headlines that roused the community. Mothers organized protest marches. With children in tow, the mothers paraded carrying eloquent placards asserting their love for the little ones in the community. The children were called "pawns" by many, and "emissaries of goodwill" by a few. Pandora's box of racial tensions had been pried open, and dark clouds of dissentious fear obscured the light of reason.

A small group of white parents formed a Concerned Citizens Committee to share opinions and seek enlightenment. Some of the members had grown up in rural communities and had been bused to school all their lives. Some of their children were bused to nursery schools. To these parents the bus ride did not seem to be the real issue. Therefore they decided to volunteer their children to be bused to a black-ghetto school as a decisive gesture of humaneness. A small minority of black parents joined in the brotherhood endeavor, and this action became a part of the temporary compliance compromise. Volunteered and selected black children were to be cross-bused to schools in all-white neighborhoods.

I had been involved in various human relations activities through the years. My imagination was caught by the drama of the quixotic school situation; I wanted to be a part of it. I had already taken a year's leave of absence from my post as an elementary education instructor at a small college to spend a year in graduate school studying open-classroom approaches. I wondered if these methods would be effective in providing significant learning opportunities for America's vast untapped natural resource—the children who do not learn well in middle-class-oriented schools. It had been five years since I had been directly responsible for an elementary school classroom. My past teaching experiences included brief stints at music teaching, special education classes —both for the hard-of-hearing and for the gifted—regular classes, three years as an elementary school counselor, and two years as a college instructor. I wanted to be back with the "shock troops who sweat and feel the rub of the harness." (A description used by a favorite author-teacher, Alice Lee Humphreys, in *Three Hear the Bells*.) I envisioned myself opening a classroom in the newly integrated school in the ghetto.

After I had spent one semester studying open-classroom theories from the ivy tower, my impossible dream came true—I was given the opportunity to teach a second-grade class in a large Midwestern city in what I will call the New School. The personnel director said,

"It'll be a challenge!" I replied, "That's what I want!"

The principal of the school didn't tell me much when I inquired about the class. "They're just children," she said with a pleading lilt to her voice.

When I entered Room 2 that Monday in January, I found a group of second-graders who had spent the past four months unnerving two previous teachers. They had become amazingly sophisticated in devising ways to make "teacher lose her cool."

Part One

The Way It Was at First

Child

Looking

Seeing himself

Reflected in broken mirrors

Troubled

Teacher

Seeking

Finding herself

Rejected by those she would help

Troubled

Part One

The Way It Was at First

PREPARATION

I looked forward to the privilege of working in the New School. I would be a part of the fascinating brotherhood thrust, and the principal supported my plans to try more open approaches. "Several teachers in the primary wing are experimenting with learning centers," she said with a wide smile. "They are expecting help from you." I felt welcomed and encouraged.

I spent most of my Christmas vacation preparing materials and arranging room furniture into activity-based learning centers. I had seen enterprising teachers do wondrous things with refrigerator packing boxes and other useful discards, but my circumstantially limited time for preparation forced me to use the standard issue equipment. Disregarding historical mind-sets about how classrooms should look, I rearranged the room. Bookcases became room dividers; the backs served as accessible bulletin boards for children's displays, and the shelves housed multimaterials for each learning center's labeled activities.

I raided the bulging teacher's closet for items of arithmetical significance. These objects along with games, including checkers and dominoes, were placed on the display shelves in the math center. A flannel board was decorated with colorful geometric cutouts that spelled a coded "welcome back to school" message.

The art center consisted of a table covered with oilcloth, cans of clay, sacks of assorted fabrics, and shelves of available paper, scissors, paints, and, as time went on, eggshells, popcorn, toothpicks, cotton, and various other alluring tidbits for collage construction. Since it was January, I succumbed to the lure of the "seasonal curriculum" and tacked up a chart illustrating six steps to cutting a happy snowflake.

The reading center included a low table and a wide assortment of books. We acquired a used rug later. I planned to bring a rocking chair and several cushions. This part of the room was to be reserved for quiet concentration.

I designed a science area around a display of labeled rocks already present. I rounded up odds and ends of science-related equipment, set some of it up, and printed enticing signs: "Can you follow the pictured directions [schematic drawing of an electric circuit] and make the bell ring?" "What happens when you mix soda and vinegar?" The children were encouraged to record their discoveries.

The listening center, with cassette player and headphones, doubled as a language arts area. There was a small store of tapes and a file of work sheets, assorted puzzle pages, rebus stories, hidden-picture games, and other paper and pencil inducements selected mainly from back issues of children's magazines (such as *Highlights*), to engender thinking and doing.

I recorded *Sounds of Laughter, Sounds of Numbers,* and *Sounds Around the Clock* from the seductive *Sounds of Language Readers* [1] collection by Bill Martin, Jr. After the animated story presentation the children could select a follow-up activity: Why wouldn't the "funny old cow" moo? How would you feel if you were the "funny old woman" or the "funny old man"? (Draw a picture if you like.) List the words that told how they felt. List the words that told how they acted. (You may draw stick people doing the actions.)

Teacher's manuals that accompany the various reading series are full of useful ideas. I modified, amplified, or minified most of the suggestions to fit the needs of a given group.

The language arts area was also equipped with camouflaged learning devices—Word Lotto, Phonics Rummy and other match-the-word picture card games, and homemade variations of Candyland and Uncle Wiggily, read-the-card-and-proceed-as-directed favorites.

Since there were to be only twenty-one students (fourteen boys and seven girls), there would be room for centers as well as for individual desks. Most of the models for open-classroom learning centers that I studied did not include individual desks. The children were free to move from one activity center to another. For sedentary activities, tables and chairs were available instead of desks. Being a midyear newcomer I didn't have time or funds to construct cubbyholes or lockers to store children's personal belongings. I have since seen some ingenious uses made of discarded locker-room baskets, shirt or shoe boxes covered with adhesive-backed paper, and plastic dishpans.

As it turned out, we called our desks "offices" and developed the idea that our desks were extensions of private space which no one could invade without invitation. The offices became temporary havens for children who needed a private place.

I didn't expect to become an instant disciple of open-classroom methodology; I did want to make an acutely conscious effort to become sensitized to the needs of the children. I started the job with a tempered sense of mission and characteristic zeal—which someone defined as a "nervous affliction affecting the young and inexperienced." (I was neither.) I intended to loosen the reins and allow the children genuine freedom to learn.

As an elementary school counselor I had taught human relations classes to many notoriously disruptive groups, utilizing hand puppets, my best dramatic ability, and great doses of empathy to win the children. I usually left such classes basking in a warm glow of presumed success. My previous experiences as an elementary classroom teacher had been characterized by equanimity. My pupils translated their positive feelings toward school into acceptable behavior. I honestly believed that I could subtly "manipulate" young children's behavior in almost any classroom situation.

The First Day went rather well. Two thirds of the class were in attendance—six Caucasians who rode the bus and eight Afro-Americans who lived in the neighborhood. The routine of getting back to school had to be reestablished for some of the children.

We started the day with a circle discussion group after

the manner of class meetings described by William Glasser in *Schools Without Failure*.[2] The children were warily polite and stoically nonresponsive to my animated overtures. In an attempt to elicit some spontaneity I started the circle conversation with the question, "If your Christmas toys could come to life, what do you think they would say to you?"

The children seemed interested in the topic, but the response was restrained. A few of the children seemed to catch the imaginative spirit of the questions but were not sure about the "right answers."

With this much encouragement I continued according to my general plans. I wanted the children to help formulate our classroom rules (standards, limits). The children agreed that the following rules were fair: Only one person could leave the room at a time. (They would check out by hanging their name tags on an "out" board.) Only one person could speak at a time during class discussions. (I went into a playful pantomime depicting how I had been trying for years to adjust my antennae so I could tune in on more than one station at a time. This was greeted with subdued laughter, mingled with puzzled looks that seemed to say, Is this how a teacher should act?)

We talked about when we should mind our own business and how we could keep from bothering ("meddlin'") people. "This is your classroom, and it will be as happy as we can make it," I declared generously. I should have said *our* classroom, for it was soon evident that their idea of an achieving, creative classroom didn't always coincide with mine.

For the remainder of the first day the children kept

occupied at the activity centers while I held individual inventory conferences. The results of the inventories revealed an overwhelming expanse of heterogeneity—pre-primer to fifth-grade achievement levels! It was going to be a challenge (an administrative synonym for a nearly impossible task!).

Except for a few minor altercations at the activity centers, the first day proceeded smoothly. I smiled a lot and was rewarded with a one-day honeymoon. The principal passed by several times and appeared relieved to see the children busily engaged. Mrs. Hershey's "controlled freedom" appeared to be working.

After school several teachers inquired about the day.

"That's a wild bunch of kids," one stated emphatically.

"How'd it go?" another asked empathically.

"That group's never learned how to mind," a third said definitively.

"You survived?" a fourth inquired sympathetically.

Not quite smugly, I replied, "The day really went very well."

"The troublemakers weren't there. Wait until tomorrow," prophesied a wise one, not quite smugly.

FRUSTRATION I

Tomorrow came. The first annoying omen: the lock on my skirt refused to function after I got to school. Was this to be a full-fledged *Test The Teacher* day? I greeted the students as they came in, made positive comments about their appearance, and recounted yesterday's joys— smiling all the while.

·

In my first-day eagerness to get things off to an effective beginning, I had forgotten about the flag salute. The second day I remembered. I asked the children to repeat the pledge, expecting the usual perfunctory performance. The droning response had just begun when it was joined by some discordant sounds from the back of the room. It seemed that Peter was putting on a show of his own. The wise teacher's prophecy was coming to pass—the honeymoon was over. The flag salute disturbance was a trial balloon sent up by the rebel forces.

To ignore or not to ignore? a pedagogical question seldom mentioned in college methods courses.

"and to the republic for which it stands, . . ."

I could hear Professor Mentor intone: "A teacher sets the stage the first day. If you let the children get by with a little, they'll try to get by with more and more." I had always considered that fallacious reasoning and wanted to prove it wrong. As a nineteen-year-old beginning teacher I had intuitively acted on the premises of "self-fulfilling prophecy."

"one nation under God, indivisible, . . ."

Professor Mentor's warnings were interwoven with flashes of countless teachers scolding children for discourteous behavior.

"with liberty and justice for all."

Derisive black faces joined the rebellious white ones in the hilarity of the moment—teacher, flag, country, forgotten.

If the ringleader hadn't been a child who had parroted

such pious phrases about cooperation the day before, I might have made the wiser choice—to ignore, and take up another activity. (Could this precocious young one have already begun to question "liberty and justice for all" as he daily boarded the bus at his comfortable middle-class home and rode to a neighborhood with unquestionable indications of poverty?)

Professor Mentor would have been proud of my little lecture to Peter on how and why we behave courteously during the flag salute. But Peter wasn't intimidated, and he chose to dispute my logic while carefully weighing the effect of his words on his peers. I was striving to keep my cool and the children were beginning to enjoy my discomfort. It was too late to retreat and I didn't want to advance. My value system could not tolerate the threatening "Do as I Say or Else" approach. But I had forced a confrontation (a tactical error) and started a "war." Nothing in my past teaching experience prepared me for this. The children chose sides and were ready for battle. There were a few neutral ones, but I had no allied support.

"Hey," I wanted to shout, "I'm your smiling teacher, the one who will trust you and let you make decisions. We're going to plan together, play together, and learn to love one another. Listen to me!"

I sensed the rumblings of further rebellion, so instead of a mini-lecture leading into an anticipated class meeting, I announced free-choice time at the activity centers so I could speak privately to Peter, expecting to level things out on a one-to-one basis. I could have been talking to a deaf-mute.

In the meantime there were several fights at the activity centers. Recess came as a welcome relief. I went out on the playground to play with the children, hoping to establish some trusting relationships. When the summoning bell rang I noticed Kent standing in a catatonic stance murmuring invectives.

"What's the matter, Kent?" I asked gently.

He looked through me and repeated, "That is a G__ d_____ m_____ f_____ bell!"

I was grateful for the subcultural exchange sessions held last semester in which we prissy white types were exposed to language that would have sent my mother scurrying for soap to scour my mouth.

"I'm sorry you feel that way, Kent," I philosophized without wincing, "but there are some things we just have to do." I took his hand and led him into the schoolhouse.

It took me several weeks to adjust to lining up the children and leading them in from the playground. I have never been much for lines. Sometimes the children from Room 2 were stopped and questioned by other teachers as they ambled through the neutralizing zones: "Whose room are you in? . . . Mrs. Hershey's? O.K., go on." The teachers were patient with this slow-learning newcomer.

Kent and I had established a reasonably friendly association by the time we reached our room. As we entered Room 2, I could understand the reason for neutralizing tactics such as calmly lining children up and leading them gently to their rooms. We were greeted by a full-scale melee.

Peter's mother and little sister had come to visit. Mrs. Love was a beloved room mother, and the children's delight in seeing her, coupled with their uncertainty about limits, exploded into a veritable chaos. Brad was sobbing hysterically while pointing a bloody hand at Denver, "He pushed me on the rocks." Several girls were doing an animated hootchy-kootchy amid a flurry of flying balls and beanbags. A dusky, angelic-looking boy was showing off a penis he had fashioned out of clay. Teacher drew deeply on her reserve of patience, focused her eyes into hypnotic balls of fire, forced her voice into its steeliest timbre, and enunciated clearly, "TAKE YOUR SEATS THIS MINUTE!" Not a speck of vulnerability showed—no soft edges of uncertainty to be taken advantage of by the doubters.

The cool, hard emergency stance worked. The children took their seats, not meekly, but quickly. I rushed the wounded hand to the health room, applied Band-Aids to the minor cuts, and hurried back to the classroom. The children had remained seated, so I grabbed a book and read a story with my best dramatic flourishes. Praise Allah, the children listened attentively until the noon dismissal bell rang.

Mrs. Love declared that a miracle had been wrought. If she only knew how hard I had struggled to hold back tears of dismay when I entered the classroom and saw the panorama of misguided energies.

I decided to try a class meeting after lunch. Maybe we could begin to verbalize some of our problems. In an attempt to rekindle sparks of imaginative interest that I had noted in our first class meeting, I used a similar opening question. "What do you think would happen if our pets could talk our language?"

The children listened fairly attentively while Butch, with lungs of iron, told about dogs he had known. At that time Butch showed no willingness to listen to any-one else. Peter, self-appointed critic, soon tired of the monologue and started a game of one-upmanship with Butch. The other children began to scrape their chairs, quite likely acting out of boredom and indifference.

I should have picked up the clues and aborted the dialogue. Instead I tried to draw out Dana, who was capable of a significant contribution, and I lost the group completely. Several of the anxious ones fell off their chairs in an all-out bid for attention. Butch asserted his authority by beating up Reggie, who had placed bubble gum on Jay's chair. (Butch had assumed protective rights over Jay, who cried easily and was often the butt of sadistic jokes.) Jay was crying because he couldn't get the gum off his pants. Torrance was chasing Janie, who had kicked him. Picture a small-scale riot! The teacher once again resorted to raucous enunciation: "I'll give you till the count of five to get to your seats!" Several waited until the count of four before they made a last-second dash for their "offices." I delved into my supply of high-interest work sheets. For the nonreaders I had dot-to-dot pictures and design-completion sheets. For the readers I had various word puzzles and riddle-type problems. When the children were given materials that they were capable of working with minimal help, they settled down and worked fairly diligently to the limits of their differing attention spans. (I have labeled this strategy "sandbagging.")

In retrospect I can list some dubious victories for law and order that second day, but it was a total personal disaster. My professional pride and my tender ego wanted to retreat and lick their respective wounds. I had

had such optimistic expectations. I thought I could establish instant rapport and facilitate a self-directed classroom in two days.

After school the second day, my fellow teachers saw a broken spirit. Nothing was said, but eyes revealed understanding, with just a touch of smugness. Faculty lounge (boiler room) comments on ensuing days:

"When you came you looked so fresh and talked so optimistically, but we knew it couldn't last."

"It's given us great comfort to know that you're having problems too."

These statements were not made maliciously. They were candid observations of things as they were. The fact that a teacher with my background was having frustrating times added credibility to their conclusion: "If *you're* having serious trouble with these children, the circumstances must be pretty rough. . . . Maybe we're not doing too badly."

FRUSTRATION II

The hostility level of these children was near 212 degrees daily. Fighting was almost a reflexive action. Many times during the first weeks the children would be busily engaged in constructive activities when the calm would be shattered by loud cries of, "He's meddlin' me," and all semblance of order would dissipate. If the protagonists went into what I dubbed the "rooster strut," the spectators would gather around to ogle and egg on, "A fight, a fight!" The adversaries would lock eyeballs, raise one shoulder, and mark out a prescribed arc with their feet as they inched closer to each other.

Sometimes the hypnotic stance was broken when one of the children would hurl a final insult and walk away. Other times the stance erupted into a clash of bodies. My mother-hen instincts led me to separate the pugilists and set them to diverse tasks. Sometimes they were asked to sit at their respective thinking desks until they could control themselves. They were allowed to vent their hostilities on clay. (Supplies for a room such as ours should include a boxing bag and plenty of boards, hammers, and nails.)

Once when I interrupted a fight on the playground, Kent would not be diverted, not even to run a race with me, knowing he would win. "I gotta get my licks back," he insisted. Impulsively I put out my hands and invited, "Here, take out your licks on my hands," expecting token slaps. I should have sent him in to use the kindergarten teacher's mad bag. My hands stung all day from the angry blows.

I was determined to carry out my deep conviction that people are not for hitting, knowing that this belief would be tested and tried. When the principal, a princess of a person, black and regally warmhearted, remarked that spanking a deserving eight-year-old might be a way of showing that one cares, I tried to reconsider the issue in the light of the subculture milieu. I couldn't bring myself to carry out a spanking even when my patience was exhausted and the level of my hostility was high enough to commit aggression. I would at times give a balky child a token swat on the lower backside. (This was taken seriously only after the children developed an honest respect for my opinions.)

Mrs. White, the principal, used the spanking option sparingly, only as a first-aid measure. She urged her teachers to work incessantly toward building a positive self-image so that the children could begin to act from a sense of self-worth. I have always believed that when a teacher sends a child she can't handle to the principal, she has admitted defeat. I couldn't do that. Sometimes I took an obstreperous child to the bench outside the principal's office until he or she calmed down. "Interstate crimes," those in which children from other rooms were involved, were always handled by the principal.

Mrs. White came for Butch after he had been involved in an interroom playground fracas. He started to object as soon as he saw her. "You ain't gonna lay your hands on me. My momma'll come to this school and tear it apart. She'll kill you!" He glanced at me. "And you too!" He didn't stop his remonstrating until he was taken to the boiler room and received several resounding swats.

When he came back to the room, he slipped into his seat and handled his humiliation by keeping his head on his desk for the rest of the day. I will have to admit that when Butch was out of commission, the other children were less restive, but I could see no positive change in his behavior after his chastising.

I do not want to give the impression that I never lost control. I resorted to physical "abuse" twice in my teaching tenure. These regrettable actions were unpremeditated, angry retorts impulsively administered. The first incident involved a child I had taught in a music class. Joe was a disturbed thirteen-year-old who had been placed in a class for the mentally retarded, a decision based on emotional retardation rather than on mental defectiveness. The teacher of this class had amazing rapport with these children. We had worked out an arrangement whereby he taught physical education to my class, a group of accelerated learners, while I taught music to his group of slow learners. This group of students balked at giving me any of the allegiance they had reserved for Mr. Strong.

The slapping incident occurred on the playground when I intervened on behalf of a younger child who was receiving angry blows from Joe. I held his arms in a viselike grip and he took out his vexation on me in a torrent of unprintables. I slapped him—with a gloved hand. He hadn't expected that and he ran into the building as though the Wicked Witch of the West herself were after him. I followed him to his room, where he sat at his desk, lividly angry, struggling with tears.

"I'm sorry, Joe, slapping you won't teach you to quit hitting others. We'll have to think of a better way. Will you accept my apology?" He nodded, seemingly stunned that I would apologize. We sat there in silence until the bell rang. I went back to my class—a safe haven of conforming high achievers, and Mr. Strong, the compassionate male figure, returned to guide Joe and his kindred.

My second loss of arm control was less forgivable. I usually disciplined with civility and touches of élan. To have resorted to the mundane and barbaric really stung my pride. I suppose that very pride needed working through.

Torrance, a child who changed his moods the way a chameleon changes color, was the victim. He wore his pride like a priceless burnous, haughtily wrapping it around him if he thought it was up for barter. He would often refuse treats brought to school by this well-meaning

white teacher. I could picture him in royal regalia resisting compromise even though the treasury was barren,
choosing starvation over humiliation. In this life he had
not been born to the ruling class, and his actions often
manifested an arrogant resentment that lashed out at any
hint of injustice. On some occasions he allowed me a
peek at a warm and sensitive soul, but mistrust of my
motives generally guided his reactions.

The day of our altercation started out unusually well,
and I allowed my expectations to soar to unseemly
heights. A timely day for good behavior, I thought, since
VIP visitors were expected. As it turned out, my anxious
desire for model behavior and the stimulation of the
presence of visitors was more than some of the children could handle. I spent most of the day trying subtly
to douse little brush fires of anxiety while maintaining a
gracious demeanor for the visitors.

By the end of the day my emotional bucket was practically drained, and the children closed in like vultures
to empty the last drop. I was still considered the enemy,
and a sign of weakness on my part elicited no sympathy.
It was an indication of vulnerability—a signal to attack.
My friendly overtures were interpreted as "She's a soft,
pushover 'enemy.'" The connotation of the "enemy"
image was almost more than I could bear.

Why couldn't the children sense the sincerity of my
actions? Weren't children and animals supposed to have
an intuitive sense about these things? I knew that the
children didn't feel good about their obstreperous behavior, but what should they do with their accumulation
of bad feelings? Those who act out their feelings generally have better mental health than those who quietly

conform, I reassured myself as I drove home after school with my empty bucket.

On the day my reserve of patience gave out, Torrance was on a tear. As usual his victim was Janie.

"Torrance is meddlin' me," she wailed for the nth time.

"Torrance, take your seat, and please stay there until the bell rings," I commanded.

"You can't make me," he retorted angrily. "You're always picking on me. Why don't you tell Peter to take his seat? He's bothering people too."

"That's probably true, Torrance, but we're talking about your problem now, so take your seat," I replied testily. If only he hadn't chosen that moment to throw the darts that smarted most. "You're just an old, white honkey," and he murmured some indistinguishable syllables. I slapped his cheek. He kicked at me and scratched my arm in his rage. I slapped him some more. Now I was justifying my action as "stopping his hysteria." Finally I held his arms tightly and led him to the principal's office to protect both of us. She wasn't in, so I asked him to stay there. His silence spoke volumes of cold fury.

I rushed back to the room and passed Mrs. Love in the hall. She looked questioningly at my shaken condition. "I hate myself for that," I exclaimed and hurried into the room. I told the class the obvious fact that teachers lose their cool too and dismissed them a few minutes early. As the children left the room I stood at the door, trying to look composed, and wished them a happy weekend. Peter was the last child to leave and his eyes showed flecks of uncertainty that I was unable to read.

I entered the principal's office just as she came in. The lingering, compassionate glance she gave Torrance told me where her sympathies lay. "You're hurting, aren't you," she stated as she saw Torrance holding his cheek. She was not referring to physical injury. She looked at me for an explanation.

"Torrance and I had some difficulties," I explained haltingly. "I lost my cool when he provoked me, and—I —I slapped him. I have no excuses for that action. I think I should take him home and explain the situation to his mother."

I had visited a number of homes in the neighborhood, but I hadn't made it to Torrance's home, and Mrs. Rose had not attended any of the parents meetings. I had no idea what kind of reception to expect. In one of Torrance's earlier rages he had told me that his mother was going to shoot me, a statement which I ignored, and on that more fortunate day, he appeared grinning at my side a few hours later offering to help me clean up after school. I loved that child and I think he knew it. Maybe that is why he felt he could safely vent accumulated venom on me, and why my striking him made him so hurt and angry.

I accepted the principal's offer to take us to the apartment complex where Torrance lived. I don't recall just what I said to Mrs. Rose when we got there, but I know she sensed my chagrin and my concern. Neither she nor Mrs. White let me feel that my actions were justified, even though they admitted that Torrance could "try the patience of Job." Nor did they condemn me. I felt accepted as a struggling fellow human being, and this acceptance kept me from too much self-recrimination.

By Monday, I could almost forgive myself, and when Torrance entered the room smiling and open-faced we let the past experiences sink into oblivion. Wasn't this a new day—the first day of the rest of our lives?

My husband, who is an elementary school principal, and my two teen-age sons can attest to the fact that many nights I came home so emotionally and physically exhausted after a day's coping that all I could do was flop on the bed and cry before I could regain sufficient revitalization to fix supper and spend several hours in preparation for another day of teaching.

I did not have a backlog of appropriate materials to stock the centers and fill packets. The adopted standardized textbooks, written for mythical middle-class children in outer suburbia, met a few needs of three or four children. Sometimes I'd be "psyched" into believing that I could ask twenty-one unique individuals with a six-year ability span to get out a "textbook" and read a lesson. I tried it several times with the second-grade science book —a well-illustrated text.

One day when the vibrations seemed conducive to mass concentration, I picked a chapter that should have interested seven- to nine-year-olds, entitled "Animal Tracks." We read a page and discussed it. I asked the gamut of "skillful questions" designed to stimulate responses from diverse mental abilities: the factual question for the encyclopedic mind, the probing question for the reluctant thinker, the divergent question for the creative thinker. After three pages of this carrying-on, the nonreaders were looking for action, the fast readers were bored, and the unmotivated average readers were looking out of the window. I decided to put more effort into setting up activities at the science center. Fortunately the school had several excellent science kits purchased with Title I money.

When I first came to Room 2 the children spent an inordinate amount of time filling in pages in their arithmetic workbooks. The workbooks were neatly programmed packages. The contents had been carefully selected in keeping with the spiral curriculum theory: "The foundations of any subject may be taught to anybody at any age in some form." [3] I agreed with the theory, but for too long curriculum supervisors seem to have operated on the naïve assumption that placing manuals in the hands of teachers and textbooks in the hands of children constitutes "curriculum" and hence "learning."

Except for about five children who happened to fit the curricular "pants," the children were using the workbooks as vehicles in a status struggle. They were involved in a race to see who could finish the arithmetic book first. The few serious math students were painstakingly working each page, asking for help as they needed it, while the others were painlessly copying the answers from filched workbooks or having big sister work the pages. After I convinced the plagiarists that I was not going to grade their books or give any other reward for first place, the competition lost its incentive, and we began to use the efficiently sequenced workbooks for meaningful learning experiences.

All but two or three students discovered that thinking felt much better than copying. The remaining copiers were totally incapable of working the material, so I legitimatized the copying by telling the children that they could copy the numbers as practice drills if they wanted to. I made sure that those children had many experiences with concrete materials.

Stan conscientiously completed his workbook a month before school was out. He had a relentless drive to excel. Workbooks challenged him and he could learn in this abstract manner. His "distractions" were always external —the noise of the children, their inattentiveness. He had trouble masking his impatience with the other children, for only Dana could begin to match his academic excellence. After one particularly trying day when he was plagued with requests for help (he had been elected student teacher), he confided in exasperation, "Those kids are stupid!" I realized then that he was tired of using so much of his time to help the other children. (The idea of the gifted students sharing their talents with the less endowed ones has merit, but it also has limits.) I arranged with the third-grade teacher for Stan to join several of her classes. She was an "old school" teacher who kept children occupied at their seats or in closely supervised groups all day. She had some marvelous gifts to share. She loved poetry and had the children memorize selected favorites. Stan enjoyed this and the relative peace and quiet of that room was soothing to him. He kept track of his schedule and would slip in and out without bothering anyone. The children hardly noticed when he was gone.

Stan was the undisputed academic champion, but his physical prowess was constantly challenged by the black boys. Although he was small, his wiry frame and relentless drive proved a match for the sturdier boys on the playing field. Generally he could outrun his companions in their favorite competitive sport—a motley version of keep-away, soccer, and football. The competition was racial as well as physical, but there were amazingly few fights while this game was in progress—except when Kent, J.B., or Jay joined in. They didn't play according to the unwritten rules, so they were kicked off the team. I would generally alternate my recess time playing kickball with the ostracized ones and jumping rope with the girls. I tried to organize games during physical education period but met with the same frustration I had in the classroom—the children would not listen to directions. Dodge ball, work-up softball, relay races, and variations of Two Deep and Run for Your Supper were sometimes successful. It was only after things got better in the classroom that things got better on the playground.

SERENDIPITY I

On the basis of my past experience, it seemed to me that my progress in gaining the trust of these children was painfully slow. So many of them had already conceded failure in the game of trying to succeed according to school rules. About one fourth of this group had failed ("flunked" in their terms) at least one year. For years, research findings have indicated that failing a child will not help him to succeed. How can failure teach success? Fortunately, the spirit of survival is strong in these children.

Some of these strong spirits maintained their identity by making up their own unwritten rules for survival. Loosely summarized, most of their actions fell into the following patterns:

1. Play deaf. You simply don't hear what the teacher says.

2. Never have a pencil, especially when the teacher gives a written assignment.

3. Leave the room frequently. Use any excuse that works.

After coping with these well-executed defense mechanisms I was beginning to comprehend why some of the teachers who had little understanding of the subculture influences resorted to super-censor, policing tactics. What defense mechanisms could a teacher use? After much introspection I had to admit that none could be justified. I couldn't blame the children. They were victims of their distorted self-perceptions. Their refusal to play the school game when they knew they couldn't win indicated a basic faith in self—a spark of hope that I had to learn to kindle. I couldn't blame myself for not having the wisdom to handle each situation with expertise. I was learning.

One exceedingly windy day several venturesome boys and I braved the elements and went out onto the playground, and I suggested a game of Chinese Tag. As I was being chased by the pack and pushed by the wind, I lost my balance and fell, grazing my knees on some rocks. The pain and my ruined hose were acceptable prices to pay for the relief I felt when I saw the concerned faces of the children. Maybe I was no longer the "enemy." I took a risk: "Will someone help me up?" Several eager arms of varying pigmentations reached down, pulled me to my feet, and helped me into the school. J.B. was especially solicitous and insisted on accompanying me to the health room to bandage my wounds. The next day Tim sidled up to me and whispered, "J.B. says he's going to marry you."

We were beginning to experience longer periods of peaceful coexistence. The cool war was practically forgotten when we were engrossed in activities that had little association in the children's minds with how things are "spozed to be" in school. Although the barriers of societal roles were still in evidence, they weren't as menacing as they had been. We were beginning to relate to one another as fellow human beings. Indications of this serendipity first became evident in the hours we called free-choice time.

There were times when the barometer readings, courses of the planets, and anything else that affects the behavior of children produced days which thwarted the best intentions of the sunniest teachers. One particularly vexing T.T.T. day my reserve of patience was rapidly being depleted. Knowing I could not resort to harsh punitive measures—physically or otherwise—I told the children I was leaving the room and would not come back until they were ready to settle down and listen to some directions. There were times when mini-lectures had to be given—edicts from the principal, directions for fire drills and other emergencies. I took courage from my feeling that I had won the basic goodwill of the children, although it had not reached the stage of having very much effect on behavior modification. I decided to test the new climate: "It's impossible for me to talk to you when you do not pay attention. I'm going to leave the room until you are ready to listen to me," I announced coolly and walked out. My intention was to demonstrate dramatically that being good for my sake was not the issue, but rather that being good for their own sakes was the crux of the whole matter. I wanted them to learn to respond to the question, Is what you are doing helping you or anyone else?

As I left the room and closed the door to stand outside, the spirits of teachers past clamored, "You've stretched trust too far too fast."

"If I had stayed in there I would have become very defensive, spelled p-u-n-i-t-i-v-e," I retorted.

"You haven't asserted your authority firmly enough. They think you're soft," whispered shades of Mentor's ghost.

"I can't be a policewoman. A cat-o'-nine-tails used every hour on the hour wouldn't make these children conform. Punishment is like an addiction—the more you use it the more it's needed," I replied.

"You've been trying your soft discipline approach for several weeks. What makes you think it will work this time?" queried the phantoms of despair—past, present, and future.

"Punishment just keeps 'evil' from showing. There's no surge of anti-life in children that has to be purged away," I went on, warming to the subject, trying to cover my apprehensions.

"You can come in now, Mrs. Hershey, we're goin' to listen to you." It was J.B., appointed leader of a newly organized cooperation contingent. (Maybe it is true that children will work for love until they learn to work.)

The next day another encouraging incident occurred. Teacher presentations were received best when given with the help of visual aids. I was using transparencies on the overhead projector, and while emphasizing an important point, I pounded the surface with my fist. There was instant response—the projector light went out. The impact had loosened some wires. A few weeks before, the children would have hooted in derision. That day there were immediate offers to help.

"I have 'nuf money saved to buy you a new bulb," Marcia offered.

"I know I can find another one," Peter stated with customary confidence.

They were trying to buoy *my* spirits!

I can't report that we were permanently transformed by those few minutes of grace, but we were renewed. There were more trials ahead, but I could face them with a recaptured spirit of optimism.

A few days later, when my attempt to be all things to twenty-one children seemed to be at a dead end, I glanced at my harried face in the mirror and agreed with Marcia's cutting perceptiveness, "Mrs. Hershey, some days you gits older and older."

That weekend, instead of frantically preparing more learning enticements and arranging and rearranging plans in my head, I got some extra rest and took a long, clear-eyed look at some "causes."

A LOOK AT CAUSES

The Need to Count for Something

The sensitivities of so many of the children in Room 2 had been distorted into flimsy ego-protecting mechanisms, coiled and ready to spring at the sound of unbearable negative criticism. Basic emotional needs cried out for fulfillment before the organism could attain a healthy sense of self-worth.

The aggressive acting-out behavior, which so vexed teachers, was a distortion of a creative spirit that would not be stifled. The resistance to conformity, which so upset the mores of the system, revealed an innate pride in the unique self. Aren't these traits important for the survival of the species? Hasn't it been the creative nonconformers who have broadened our vistas and turned dreams into realities?

I was well aware of the basic goodness and rightness of these children. Because I had to work with them in an institutional setting, I had to determine the extent of my compromises. To what degree could I sacrifice individual well-being for the good of the group, and to what extent could I compromise the good of the group for institutional demands?

One thing was certain, this group of second-graders would not be manipulated. Their manifesto was set forth in one of Butch's comments the first week: "Nobody is gonna make me do nothin' I don't wanna do." And in Janie's words: "That white woman ain't gonna outsmart us." (In time I earned the title of *teacher*.)

Much of the children's daily emotional sustenance seemed to come from playing a "game" of Who's Going to Be Top Man Today? The teacher wasn't a recognized player. The most powerful status challenger was the candy and gum provider. If the benefactor of sweets could share his wealth with the chosen ones without teacher interference, he scored high. The dispensing of favors was sometimes interrupted by an informer whose need for attention vied with the cravings of his sweet tooth. Then it was open parley.

At first I naïvely concluded that getting the students involved in stimulating learning games would undercut the appeal of candy bartering. No way. Resorting to my Teacher's Neat Trick bag, I announced that anyone who brought goodies to school must bring enough for the whole group. I "cruelly" confiscated the small caches and saved the contents until there was enough to go around. This strategy worked, and some children pooled their pennies to buy regular treats for the class.

The children's pervasive need for status cropped up in other disruptive endeavors. Collecting empty milk cartons became the next Top Man game. The children turned down the corners and stacked them. The boy with the highest tower of cartons was Top Man for the day. This seemed an innocuous before-school pastime. But it wasn't long before it developed into a "gangland" competition complete with strategic manuevers and raids. When it reached feuding proportions, I intervened and cleared the room of milk cartons which had been cached in every conceivable hiding place. One positive observation: the "gangs" were integrated! This would not have been the case a few weeks before.

The white children from advantaged environments (with regard to preparation for the school world) were uncomfortable in their minority role. The black children were confused by the majority role. These children, victims of decades of indifference to human dignity, were now the chosen ones in the great experiment of togetherness. The social consciences of the white parents had offered their children for the integration experiment.

The black children in Room 2 were forced to live with the awareness that the white children had superior academic backgrounds. All but two of the white children were capable of working above grade level according to prescribed curriculum guidelines.

The tongue stuck in my cheek reminds me to confirm my agnostic position regarding grade-level "norms." Nonetheless, of such is the stuff of school made, and the children were painfully aware of it.

My decision to eliminate the established apartheid reading groups in favor of individualized reading conferences was fortified by Jay's perceptive comment as he saw the five Anglo-Saxon achievers who had comprised one group gathered at the reading center: "Hey, look, Mrs. Hershey, there are Mrs. Parker's special boys." Jay had conceded failure in all academic pursuits, but his flashes of insight betrayed more ability than he chose to utilize.

Mrs. Parker, a gracious black woman who had filled in as a substitute for two months, had conscientiously organized reading and math groups. For reasons unknown to me, all the black high achievers were in the other second-grade room. However justified, the grouping reinforced all tendencies toward segregation, and certainly did not serve the purpose of the integration endeavor. I listed ability grouping as one of the causes for the high hostility level in the room.

Mrs. Parker had sounded the praises of her "achieving boys" and had held them up as examples to the low-achieving black students. I'm sure that this was done to motivate the disadvantaged ones to work harder, but "there's nothing as unequal as the equal treatment of the unequal." It was the black children's lack of standard English, school-oriented experiential background that caused the inequality in academic pursuits. This is cause for white guilt, not for black racial shame.

The cowed black children retaliated by making life as miserable as they dared for Mrs. Parker in the classroom, and as miserable as they dared for the white boys on the playground.

Most of the white parents were aware of this dichotomy and did all they could to counteract it. They volunteered to help in the classroom, took children on field trips, and invited the black children to their homes. The black children viewed the white parents as rich benefactors as well as friends. These children were gaining firsthand experience of how the other half lives. I wondered how the children reconciled the disparity in life-styles. From my observations I concluded that it reinforced the insidious white superiority theme for some. Others who had been exposed to militant rhetoric showed an absorbed resentment at being the havenots. If you have so much more than me, I must not be O.K. The subservient role was not accepted, and some concluded, If I'm not O.K., you're not O.K.[4] Racial shame and racial guilt played havoc even with the young.

In examining causes, I could not disregard my ambiguous feelings toward the melting-pot experiment. Some days I wished we could all be dyed green and start over. I had to be careful not to do a reversal of the "my boys" act and oversympathize with the underdogs. These children didn't need sympathy. What they did need was security, success, and *earned status.*

The Need to Be Unique

There are practices within the school system that are "causes" of the problems the system is supposed to solve. There are cannibalistic gremlins that nibble away at a student's self-esteem and gorge themselves on the heap of failures produced by a competitive marking system. The grade-and-label gremlins have no mercy on those who cannot keep step because, to paraphrase Thoreau, they hear the beat of another drummer.

The lockstep gremlin commands that all children learn the same prescribed amount of knowledge in nine months. Didactically interpreted, his edicts state:

> Spoon-feed six portions of the approved curriculum daily.

> Grade and label the digested material. (Little or no resemblance of this material to the original feeding is to be labeled "failure.")

There is rarely time to repeat the feedings for those who have trouble digesting the material. In order to meet state requirements, at least 1,080 portions must be laid out during the year. Those who cannot handle this amount are asked to repeat the process the next year. (It is hoped that their digestive systems will make some kind of adaptation during the intervening months.) The school public-relations people call it giving the children another chance. The children spell it f-l-u-n-k-e-d, no matter what it's called. (Only in school and in prison do we put a time limit on learning!)

The test-and-label gremlin insists that all the informa-

tion about what children know or how much they are
capable of learning can be accurately measured. This
gremlin sanctions the use of scores obtained from group-
administered I.Q. and achievement tests to determine
placement in special education rooms and other life-
shaking decisions.

A *True Testing Story*

The fourth day of the first week of the first month was
mental maturity testing day. Anyone who could read,
work a stopwatch, and follow directions could administer
the test. The tough part was to get the children to
listen to directions, follow test protocol, and put out
reasonable efforts.

The white boys, Jay excepted, decided to put forth
maximum effort after they were told that the scores
would become part of their permanent records. They
already equated the scores with college entrance and job
success. Sandy, who spoke of her ambition to be a nurse,
took pride in completing her work, and Barbara always
followed Sandy's lead. I attempted to motivate the remaining fourteen by appealing to their bona-fide digestive systems. I promised them gingerbread men and
Kool-Aid if they would do their best on the test. "As
soon as the test is finished we'll have a party," I promised.

For some, this wasn't sufficient stimulus to sustain
efforts when they discovered they didn't have a "50
percent chance of success." Kent chose to pout, and no
amount of bribery enticed him to complete the test. I
had to prod, tease, and cajole to get the remaining
thirteen to continue to mark their test books. Most of

them were guessing, not even attempting to use the thinking ability I had seen them manifest daily in informal situations. This test had no relevance to their here and now. Why should they go through the painful motions of sitting still and concentrating? (Sometimes called self-discipline—but they hadn't heard of it.)

About midmorning we took a break from test tensions and went out onto the playground. I hurried in ahead of the children and poured Kool-Aid for a quick refresher and "settle-downer." "As soon as you sharpen your pencils and take your seats, I'll bring your drink," I manipulated.

Shortly after I had started the last portion of the test I noticed that Kenyon was missing. As soon as Stan finished, I sent him to the principal's office with a note: "Kenyon's missing, and we haven't finished our mental maturity testing in Room 2. Can you help?"

Shortly before dismissal, the principal appeared at the door with Kenyon in tow—he had run home from the playground during our break. He was a Jehovah's Witness and could not attend parties, so he took off before I could serve the gingerbread men. If only I had known, I wouldn't have called our refreshments a "party."

It distresses me to think that the scores of such tests are imprinted on children's permanent records as intelligence quotients. Therefore I listed grading and blanket testing as causes for much teacher and student frustration. I viewed them as forces that produce failures and undermine the uniqueness of individuals.

I can testify to the fact that the children in Room 2 did not allow me to forget their uniqueness—each day I was reminded anew. There were times when I found myself longing for neat rows of conformers. Then I would think of an alleged statement by Thoreau to a "sage on the stage" teacher: "Lady, why do you want those children to be just like you? One of you is enough."

I found that I had to assess the priorities of each situation, balancing the weighty edicts of the system against the heavy pull of individual wills (including the times when the teacher's will pulled counter to the children's). As our personal relationships became more trusting and congenial, though the manifestations were erratic, I felt that it was possible to initiate positive strategies for change.

Part Two

What We Did to Change Things

School

Children

Exploring life

Learning the meaning of their world

Teachers

Exploring life

Learning the meaning of their world

Children

Part Two

What We Did to Change Things

HUMANIZED RELATIONS

I used the bucket analogy with the children to help them to understand some of the mysteries of human relations. I was introduced to the bucket metaphor in a speech given by Dr. Donald Clifton [5] of the University of Nebraska. It made a lasting impression on me and I have used it as an object lesson with scores of children and adults. Feeling really good about oneself is synonymous with a full bucket. When that is the case, a person can give of his fullness and fill someone else's bucket. "You really know how to hit the ball!" "You do wonders for that suit!" An empty bucket denotes bad feelings about ourselves, and we dip into the bucket of another person in an attempt to fill our own emptiness. "You missed the ball as usual." "That color makes you look sick." Our dipper may empty another's bucket, but it develops a leak on the way back to our own bucket, so neither bucket is filled. When we fill another person's bucket, something magical happens—our bucket becomes fuller too!

The children readily picked up the essence of the analogy, and some were able to use it as an alternative to fist-swinging: "Hey, you're emptying my bucket!" (Much less complicated than fighting.) It seemed that the phenomenon of "emptying" had to be thoroughly explored before we could concentrate on "filling."

The black children's densely peopled environment had engendered in them a highly sensitized awareness of human needs. Their ability to read nonverbal clues was uncannily accurate. They were able to detect when I was just "jivin'" and when my rhetoric would result in action. If their insights could be matched with appropriate jargon, I am sure we would be amazed at their psychological astuteness. Unfortunately their sensitivities were too often distorted, turned inward like an ingrown toenail to grow sore and to fester. How can one fill another's bucket when one's own is always empty?

I used Ojemann materials [6] for class discussions on human relations. "Why do people act as they do?" is the basic question pursued by the invaluable collection of relevant stories and activities. A story that elicited an insightful response from Debra involved Bobo,[7] a monkey without a tail, who was constantly bothering his peers and disrupting meaningful monkey activities. The children's attention was captured, and they identified with the tailless monkey's antics. I stopped at various points in the story and questioned the children about their reactions, probing for feeling-level responses. I asked them to help solve problems as they arose in the context of the story. "What do you think the worried Keeper should do to help Bobo?" I asked.

"Teach him to do somethin' real good," Debra responded as though prompted by Dr. Ojemann himself.

I will never stop marveling at the pristine wisdom of children. School had already labeled Debra a failure. She had repeated a grade and had shown minimal progress in academic subjects since then. According to the school psychologist, Debra had definite perceptual problems, and the school nurse reported a hereditary blood disease. I couldn't fail her. What could I teach her to do "real good"?

One important factor in Debra's favor was that she was well accepted by her peers. She had "spirit" as well as "soul." Sometimes she seemed bent on exposing every phony element in the process of education. I couldn't always view her disruptiveness charitably; some days she appeared to be hell-bent on being "mean." At such times I learned to take her hand wordlessly and have her sit near me or make the learning rounds with me. She usually accepted this resignedly. After she regained her "goodness" she would go back to her tasks. I learned to leave her packet of materials (selected to help remediate her perceptual problem) on a table for her to discover, for she would rarely follow "orders."

One day I came in after recess to see her berating a cowering Kent, who was nearly a head taller than she.

"Boy, why you tear that girl's dress?" Debra demanded menacingly, referring to Tricia's freshly torn blouse.

"I didn't." Kent was backed into a corner and ready to burst with humiliation. In desperation he took off his shoe and threatened to throw it at Debra. She didn't back off one inch.

"You just fix it," she insisted.

By that time I had reached the scene and I couldn't help asking, "How should he fix it, Debra?"

"Wid his hands, jes like he tore it," she replied emphatically.

I had learned that hashing over mishaps such as this served no good purpose, so I directed my attention to the sobbing victim.

"My mamma will spank me when she sees my new blouse is torn," Tricia lamented, clutching the bow that had been torn off leaving an ugly gash in the material. I assured her I would sew it up after school, and it would be almost as good as new.

Kent finally muttered a coerced, "I'm sorry," and Debra took her seat triumphantly.

Accumulated injustices had left their mark on these children. Integration is one attempt to heal a social disease, but was I knowledgeable enough and compassionate enough to withstand the draining of the poison? I felt I had to be. Some mornings I would drive to school telling myself that I was going to conduct group therapy sessions rather than teach school. This shift of perceptions seemed to help.

"Teacher, Janie called you a white witch." Debra's eyes gleamed in anticipation.

"I'm sorry she feels that way," I said calmly, noting I had Janie's attention.

"You mean you still like her?" Debra asked incredulously.

"Sure, I like Janie, but maybe she doesn't like herself too well today," I answered while reaching over to pull an apprehensive Janie close to me.

"Do you like yourself?" Debra queried further, with intent interest.

"Yes, most of the time. I don't always like everything

I do," I continued, wondering if this could make sense to them.

"I don't ever like myself," Debra declared, shrugging her tiny shoulders and walking off.

Several days later, after a riotous recess, I finally got the children sorted out, seated, and calmed down enough to talk with them. "What happened on the playground?" I asked in my "I mean business, I want to know" voice.

"Everybody was fightin'!" several voices claimed.

I saw no value in conducting a lengthy inquisition at that time, so I shared my feelings of disappointment. "What could have caused so many fights? I thought we had such a great morning. Everyone was so busy and happy," I chided without attempting to hide my concern. (My disapproval was beginning to have some effect on the children.)

Some of the children looked sheepish, others appeared sullen and defiant. Finally, one child decided to risk peer disapproval and level with me.

"I guess we didn't like ourselves very much," Peter offered weakly.

"That's it," Debra agreed, while other heads were nodding.

I let the anticipated discussion rest with that statement. Another time I would ask them what we could do to help ourselves to "like ourselves." Given time in a nonjudgmental atmosphere where reasonable behavior is modeled, these children can learn to make value judgments and to modify their behavior.

When the children started to believe that they had a respected voice in decision-making, they responded better in class meetings. Their cooperation was a gradual evolution, and several of the children seemed completely unable to gain anything meaningful or helpful from the sessions. I tried to conduct most of our meetings with the children seated in a circle of chairs. In time the excessive chair-scraping and peer-baiting abated.

After our first few disasters I always gave the children the option of nonparticipation. "If you do not want to be a part of our class meeting today, you may work at your desks, as long as you don't bother us." (If they bothered us anyway, they were given one warning and then asked to sit on the bench.) I don't believe that there were ever more than three or four children at a time who opted to sit out on the discussions.

I tried not to let our class meetings get into the negative rut of constantly discussing peer problems, although I was glad we were developing a viable forum for solving social problems. Some of our best discussions of social problems evolved from open-ended questions. "What would the world be like if we were all green?" was an opener one day. After the first flip comments ("We'd look funny," "We'd be sick"), the children began a serious discussion of skin pigmentation. To help them understand pigmentation, I pointed to my freckles and asked, "What color would I be if these spots were so close it would look like they covered my skin?" (I am exceedingly fair-skinned.)

"Brown!" was the unanimous exclamation.

"Like us," Julie added, and squealed with laughter.

The bell summoning us to recess called the conversation to a halt, but not before Stan concluded, "If we were all green, there would probably be shades of green."

Shades of joyous discovery! Would we deprive the children of such opportunities?

Sometimes our discussions dealt with specific problems, and this could cause discomfort.

"Miz Hershey," Butch complained one day, "the white kids always get to do more than we do."

"Tell me what you mean, Butch," I insisted.

"Well, like Stan and Dana always is doin' extra stuff we don't get to do," he continued with a glance around the circle, seeking affirmation.

"How do the rest of you feel?" I followed his glance.

"They get to do more than I do too, because I don't finish my work like they do," Peter defended with candor.

"Me too," Jay, Brad, and Tim agreed.

"You do let Stan do more stuff," Torrance chimed in.

I reminded them that they had elected Stan student teacher to help them spell words and so on, and that Dana was his assistant. I then added, "Why don't we talk about some ways we could work things out so no one would feel left out?" A few children parroted some pat responses. Butch seemed to be pacified.

I often talked with the children in terms of values, attempting to translate the word into illustrations they could comprehend. I believe that children can modify their behavior after they make a valid value judgment. As long as an adult holds a whip over a child's head, whether it be grades or other forms of coercion, the child may conform. Remove the whip and the child acts out of his value system.

I held the reins loosely and allowed the children to "stumble and pick themselves up," but they knew I had the "bandages and ointment" ready. I talked with children whose behavior constantly upset the class equilibrium and asked them if what they were doing was helping them or anyone else. If they decided it wasn't, we worked on a plan, sometimes in the form of a contract. If a child broke this commitment, I would not accept excuses. This was difficult for me, but I had heard William Glasser insist that people who care don't accept excuses, and I knew he was right. Instead, we must agree on another (more realistic) plan. The key to success is the involvement of a caring adult.

If a child could not or would not make a value judgment about his behavior, we couldn't make a plan, and the child would have to take the natural consequences of his behavior. When we talked about consequences of unacceptable behavior the children would often suggest excessively punitive procedures. Heads would nod in agreement with the little Pharisee who remarked: "If you hit someone, you ought to get spanked by the principal."

"Do you want to be sent to the principal for a spanking?" I countered.

"No way," was the instant response.

"Is there a chance you'll ever hit someone?" I probed.

"Could be," inevitably followed by downcast eyes.

"Do you think getting spanked by the principal is a good consequence?" I continued.

The answers would vary. Although spankings were dreaded, the children could think of no feasible alternatives.

"Is there anything we could do that would help us remember to use inner control and not hit someone when we are angry?" I asked rhetorically.

Dana, a thoughtful child from a home where empathy was taught and caught, offered an elegant comment. Stated the young sage: "I think when we lose our tempers we need a place to cool off and think. A spanking would just make us madder."

"Yeah, we could sit at the bad desk," Jay suggested.

"Jay, I can't accept that suggestion if you insist on calling the thinking desk a 'bad desk,'" I retorted. I had set aside an extra desk as a "thinking desk." At first, when the children would not accept any attempts to reason, I would ask a persistent meddler to sit at the desk and work out his aggressions on clay, draw a picture, or do some work sheets. I had tried to eliminate all punitive connotations from this arrangement, but Jay saw it as plain old punishment and that was "bad."

As our mutual trust grew I continued to isolate children for unacceptable behavior, but I always told them they could come back and join the group whenever they felt ready. "You may come and join us whenever you can trust your inner control." (That was another term we were beginning to understand.)

I knew that the concept was grasped by one child when Butch told me one day: "I'm leavin' the room for a while. If I stay in here, I'll bust somebody's head for sure." I nodded my approval as he left to sit on the bench in the hall until he had gained enough control to cope with his feelings of hostility. Butch's very presence carried impact. He had "street smartness" coupled with sensitivity, a charismatic combination that could not be ignored. School had already failed him. His talents did not lend themselves to the square steps of the academic curriculum, and he flunked first grade. This confirmed his suspicion, and his mother's certain conviction, that school was enemy territory. Fortunately, Butch's second experience in first grade did not verify these negative conclusions. This teacher acted on her belief that you could not make the child fit the mold, so she adjusted the mold to fit the child. Although her skin was white, she had an unusual empathy for children of all pigmentations. Butch had a tolerable year and was "passed" to second grade.

Butch entered second grade ready to give his loyalty to a teacher who would meet him halfway. Miss May was such a teacher, but she left in October to teach on an Indian reservation, a fact that Butch found hard to forgive, and was replaced by a substitute who beat out a cadence that Butch didn't dig. When I took over the class in January, Butch was a sullen dissenter living up to his "bad guy" image.

Admittedly, I devoted a lot of energy to this child. I knew I had to capitalize on his obvious leadership abilities. Sometimes he would really blow it and I would visit with him about the implications of trust and responsibility, wondering if any of it got through. My words may not have registered, but he didn't forget actions. His perceiving eyes took in all proceedings and filed them for future reference. He knew when I acted honestly and when I was jiving. He would complain vociferously of any injustices, real or inferred, but didn't fail to note when teacher was fair. He did not pick on weaklings, but delighted in tormenting his physical equals.

Denver was one of these. He was larger than Butch, but not as quick-witted. He would regularly complain that Butch was picking on him. Yet when Denver was in tears because his only coat had been torn in a recess fracas, Butch left his playing to find pins to mend the tear. The soul brother empathy was not lost on this white, middle-class teacher. I may never really understand their world, but something in me could understand their feelings and Butch knew this.

One day I brought to school the Diana Ross record *Reach Out and Touch Somebody's Hand,* and a ritual evolved. "I can't do it alone, and you can't either, we need each other," I added impulsively. Mr. Love visited that day and we went around the room shaking hands with each child. We repeated this ritual a number of times during the year.

On Friday, February 12, we celebrated Valentine's Day and Abraham Lincoln's birthday. Every child in the primary wing was given a heart on a string with "I Am Loved" on it. As each child entered Room 2, I placed the heart around his neck and shook his hand to reinforce the written words. There were no jarring vibrations that morning, and we sat on the rug and read a moving story about Abraham Lincoln.

Before I read the story I told the class that only those who wanted to listen should sit with us. All but Torrance and Butch chose to join us, and Butch listened from his desk. I read for fifteen minutes. Fearing that I had pressed attention spans to the breaking point, I closed the book and promised to finish the story later. The children insisted that I finish the book. They sat quietly absorbed in the story for nearly forty-five minutes and then discussed the implications of slavery for another ten minutes. Brad's mother was with us that day and we exchanged looks of amazement.

On the days that I was able to relax my worries about

academic achievement and relate honestly at the feeling level, there was always more cause for rejoicing. Then I would ask myself, Why have we teachers been so programmed to be hyperconscientious about the wrong things? I wonder if we could stop a healthy Johnny from reading when he is developmentally ready, *if* he feels good about himself *and* the proper stimuli are present?

> What did we see on our walking trip today? Talk, talk, talk. First the teacher writes down the children's stories. Then the children copy their stories. Write, write, write. The squiggly chicken scratches on paper come to life. "I said those words." "I will read that—I can READ!"

It is possible for a teacher to "keep school" and mechanically follow textbook plans, but there is no *joy*. As I began to lose my fears (mostly of paper tigers), I responded naturally to the spontaneous discoveries of the children. When their cups ran over with joy, I would catch some of the excess in my dipper and so fill my drained bucket.

POSITIVE REINFORCEMENT

As I worked with the children in Room 2, positive reinforcement became my constant companion. This was not synonymous with praise. Praise was accepted by the children, but mostly with shrugs. Those who didn't merit the daily role of being complimented (and knew it) reacted to praise with intensified hostility. As the children's confidence in me increased I found that an honest reflection about their work or behavior was a more effective reinforcer. For example, if a child was struggling with cursive writing and showing signs of impatience with himself, I might go to him and ask him to write his favorite letter of the alphabet. I would then share his pride in the accomplishment.

When a child who had been a persistent meddler was applying his energies to a creative task, I would try to confirm the joy of his accomplishment. If his project could be displayed or put to another useful purpose, such as reading his story to someone, putting on a play, or extending the project into a field trip, the child would be convinced that my appreciation was deeper than the superficial praise he had come to suspect. When a child brought his work to me for correction I would emphasize the right answers. Dr. Hugh Riordan,[8] spouter of wisdom, used the following exercise with teacher groups. He wrote the word "womin" on the chalkboard and asked the teachers to relate what they would say to a child who had written "women" that way on a spelling test. "I'll tell him it was wrong and show him how to spell it correctly," or "I'd tell him it sounded right spelled that way, and spell it correctly for him," were typical responses.

Dr. Riordan then queried, "Why can't we say it's four fifths *right?*"

Traditionally, school has not taught children that it is all right to make mistakes, because that is how we learn: make a mistake, correct a mistake, do it right, feel good. Doesn't that make more sense than: make a mistake, get a bad grade, feel bad, maybe never do it right? Making a mistake is then translated, "I'm a failure." It is a demeaning thing to try and try and fail and fail. Finally it is easier to stop trying.

"Most people need at least a 50 percent chance of success before they'll try a new task," Dr. Riordan stated. The child protects his ego by withdrawing or diverting his energies to other attention-getting devices. Then he can tell himself: I probably could have done that work if I'd wanted to, but who wants to read those stupid books (do those silly problems, write those boring papers)? Self-fulfilling prophecy: the child acts out of his negatively reinforced feelings. To counteract this negative spiral, I tried to make the children comfortable with their mistakes, emphasizing the process of learning over the end product.

I noticed that the children who had been labeled "failure" by being flunked were the experts in avoidance tactics. Hence the need for new strategies. Case in point: I had been giving group lessons on cursive writing. I tried to make the presentation enticing by using clever illustrations and appropriate background music. The successful children were happily forming loops and slides. Kent's posture was rigid, and his head was bent close to his paper as he labored over each stroke.

I walked over to reassure him: "You're making some nice A's; I like the way you're staying on the line."

A minute later he emitted a loud wail, crushed his paper, hurled it on the floor, and began to sob, head on arms, while mumbling: "I can't make those m_____ f_____ letters right! I'll never make them right."

I learned to leave Kent alone after outbursts like that, because the more I tried to reassure him the angrier he got. I continued to make positive comments when it seemed feasible, but cause for celebration came the day

Jay's bucket was full enough to allow him to tell Kent, "You write beautifully, Kent."

There were many long, sometimes discouraging, days between the inauguration of my positive-reinforcement program and such spontaneously effective payoffs. In the meantime I was learning that to make sense out of chaos, I had to use immediate rewards. Deferred rewards in the form of special privileges worked for very few children. Mostly these inducements were ignored or disdained as bribes. In order to make an impact I had to appeal to a top-priority item—the love of sweets. To help us survive the first few weeks, I gave out chocolate candies for all positive behaviors that came to my attention. (The children were amused by "Hershey's Kisses.") After the novelty wore off, the children responded less enthusiastically to the idea of sweet-tooth bribery. By that time I had won precious minutes of their attention, and we could begin to make some group decisions. After the third week I no longer brought chocolate crutches. We continued to have frequent refreshments, but it was in the spirit of a group celebration of learning. Until such a spirit became manifest the candy tokens and frequent educational movies helped me to survive.

When the children began to show pleasure about their improved behavior, and this self-satisfaction became a springboard for some analytical thinking, I knew we had made the precarious transition from extrinsic motivational gimmicks to the honest joys of intrinsic motivation. Joy is the supreme reinforcer, for it reflects the natural condition of the human organism.[9] (I don't think Professor Mentor would have approved of the use of joy as a reinforcer. "Children must learn that roses have thorns," she would chide.)

"Mrs. Hershey, Mrs. Hershey, come look," Jay demanded incessantly as he blossomed from the fearful class scapegoat into an assertive individual. (The "thorn" with the "blossom.") Jay required constant reinforcement. In contrast to his earlier behavior, he was now seeking it more constructively.

"That's a beautiful painting. Let's put it up," I would comment approvingly. (Art was Jay's strong point.)

"Will you be the illustrator for our class book?" I asked him one day.

"We didn't know Jay was such a good artist," the children reinforced joyfully.

PERSONALIZED INSTRUCTION

Introspection

My utopian vision of personalized instruction involved a balance of directed and semi-directed group activities along with guided and spontaneous individual pursuits. The teacher would be an active participant with the children in decision-making. Since guarding children's well-being is the teacher's responsibility, she must intervene in any situation that might undermine the welfare of the group or of an individual. This demanded the wisdom of Solomon. Lacking such a divine gift, I had to rely on a mixture of intuition, Spock, Ginott, Rogers, Glasser, *et al.*—and ofttimes on the collective wisdom of the children.

Once a week we had sing-along time in the primary wing. The children gathered in the hall for a modified pep rally designed to heighten self-awareness and enhance togetherness. The children would sing: "If you're great and you know it, clap your hands . . . nod your heads . . . stamp your feet. . . . If you're great and you know it, then your life will surely show it. If you're great and you know it, clap your hands. . . ."

On these occasions birthdays were celebrated and acts of valor recognized. Good citizen nominees were pinned with homemade badges. It was a spirited gathering which the children seemed to enjoy. Yet several boys in Room 2 balked at attending. (Maybe their sense of "not-O.K.-ness" couldn't take singing "I'm The Greatest." I had trouble with that one too.) I didn't want to insist that the boys take part, but there were school rules regarding children in unsupervised rooms. Feeling it was a safe venture in democracy, I asked the class to vote on attendance policies for school assemblies. Everyone went to sing-along—majority rule!

The children in Room 2 taught me that I could not force learning to happen. I could only work on the learning environment and on my attitude toward the children and myself. I will try to keep the accounts of my weeks of trial and error painfully accurate, in the hope that my setbacks will encourage others to continue to experiment with varied approaches of meeting children's needs while attempting to understand their wants.

Individualized Action

As I have indicated, the extent of heterogeneity and the level of hostility in this classroom made traditional teaching methods inconceivable, even if I had wanted to play the "sage on the stage" role. I directed my initial strategies (in the cool war I hadn't declared) toward initiating a frontal attack on the academic, social, and racial cliques in the room—this called for individualized action.

I used the results of individual inventories in reading and math to develop a guide for the compilation of tailored packet material. In January only thirteen out of twenty-one students were capable of following some written directions, so I had to rely on nonverbal materials for the other eight. Several of these children seemed to have perceptual difficulties—developmentally their eye and hand coordination, figure and ground perception, ability to see spatial relationships, and other visual discernments important to decoding the printed word were at the reading readiness level and below. I scoured the storage room for discarded readiness workbooks to be torn up for packet fodder, and latched on to any perceptual-training material I could find.

I launched the packet individualization attempt with the stipulation, "After you've finished the work in your packets, you may have free-choice time." During the first few days only about four children finished the assigned material in their packets before making a bee-line for the activity centers. The others did a work sheet or two that happened to appeal to them and went on to free choice at the buzzing centers. I decided against an all-out confrontation regarding incompleted work. (My T.N.T. bag didn't have a big enough ramrod.) Those whose interest and attention spans could tolerate the packet work generally checked off the items on their daily job sheet before the dismissal bell rang. The laggards required more understanding, and a revision of my expectations.

Thank goodness I didn't have to worry about the noise level. Our principal had a realistic set of educational priorities, and she supported her teachers' attempts to innovate and experiment with a variety of approaches in order to meet children's educational needs. She actually agreed that concentrating children are not bothered by noise.

I had a number of children who undoubtedly were perfecting their ability to speak by shouting down any competition. Someone has called this the "crowing game," which means, loosely interpreted, "the squeaking axle gets the grease." For the most part I attempted to counteract such cacophonous interaction by being a model of soft speech. Sometimes my internal combustion erupted and I outshouted the children. This proved effective only when used sparingly, and for announcements of utmost importance.

I have worked with many teachers who thought children could learn only when they were deathly quiet. I have often wondered how they thought children acquired the most important skill of a lifetime—the ability to speak their mother tongue. No one taught them formally, yet the children use nouns, verbs, and adjectives quite efficiently.

In addition to keeping the packets supplied with constructive sandbagging material, carefully selected to whet the appetite for "work," I continued to expand the activity center approach. I allowed varying amounts of free-choice time daily. Until our program of humanizing peer relations began to show results, one hour of self-direction was all the children could tolerate within the bounds of institutional behavior requirements. The fact that a child would lose the privilege of free choice if he couldn't conduct himself reasonably helped stretch tolerance levels. (Anything that is stretched too far will snap back!)

The last hour of the day was generally designated a free-choice hour. At that time the children desperately needed distraction from their pent-up hostilities and from their *hunger*. I gambled on the odds that children concentrate best when engaged in activities of their own choice. This proved to be true except when tempers would flare uncontrollably. Then I would direct the "free" choice and we would have a film. Watching a screen in a darkened room was soothing and educational —especially for the teacher.

Group Reaction

Generally my attempts to present a lesson to the whole group fell flat because at least half the children either wouldn't listen or couldn't comprehend. I'm sure that this is how most teacher lectures are received by young children, even in classrooms where students are too polite to be openly disruptive. Most of the children in Room 2 chose to reveal their true feelings. I persistently tried every gimmick I could think of to facilitate group listening. One day I feigned laryngitis and used sign language for a while, but before long I would have used all the neat tricks in my bag, and what then?

On days when barometer readings and other factors which seem to affect children's moods were favorable, I would take advantage of the climate and present a "model" lesson, complete with behavioral objectives. One day I gambled on atmospheric conditions. Billowing clouds of steam greeted the children as they entered the room. The clouds were rising from a pot of water boiling on a hot plate. The questions of the children led to a productive discussion on forms of water, and to the formulation of theories on how clouds are formed. I sent a child for a tray of ice cubes, and we made "rain."

After repeating the experiment with the children participating, I proceeded to review the concepts which I was sure at least 90 percent of the children had grasped, for even Butch appeared enthralled with the proceedings.

"What are clouds made of?" I asked routinely.

Butch responded without hesitation, "Clouds are made of cotton," and he wasn't trying to be funny.

I overheard Marcia say to Sandy, "I don't believe in that stuff, do you?"

During a rainstorm a few days later, less than one fourth of the class could explain the phenomenon of clouds and rain. I had expected children who, developmentally, were thinking in concrete terms to make abstract generalizations.

Many incidental science lessons got higher ratings on my unofficial concept-attainment tally sheet. Curious children could grasp concepts when explained as answers to *their* questions.

"Why is it so dark in here when we come in from the snow?" Jay wondered one wintry day. The answer included the participation of other wondering ones who were directed to "watch each other's pupils—that opening in your eye that looks like a little black ball—get larger and smaller as you close your eyes for a while and then open them." And so they covered a whole chapter in the science texts on "How Eyes Adjust to Light."

One directed multiconcept lesson that was well received by students with differing levels of comprehension called for a large box of toothpicks and assorted bottles of food coloring. The early comers that morning dyed toothpicks red, green, blue, and yellow. As other children arrived they helped to count and sort each color. I told the children that I planned to scatter the toothpicks in the grass and asked them to guess (estimate) how many of each color we would find. The children enjoyed the guessing game, and each child recorded his estimate on a sheet of paper. Several alert students caught on to the camouflage concept. The others were caught up in the competition of guessing the "right" number.

Later in the day when we needed a change from confining indoor activities, we went outdoors to hunt toothpicks, small paper cups in hand. The children were given a five-minute time limit for the hunt. When time was called they counted the number of toothpicks picked up according to color. We graphed the results.

"I told you we wouldn't find as many green ones cuz the grass'd hide 'em," Butch exulted.

Flexible Schedules

A schedule of the nonvariable events was posted on a chart in the room. Recess, library periods, and the reading teacher's schedule were listed. The remedial reading teacher worked twenty minutes a day four days a week with small groups of children who were not reading at grade level. This included all but four boys at midyear.

Each morning I would print a tentative schedule for the day on the chalkboard and go over it with the students. (As their sense of responsibility for the room increased, the quality of their participation in planning improved.) During the first half of the semester the day was divided roughly into four blocks of time: individual work time (packets to start with), organized center work time, directed group activities, and free-choice time.

Dr. Harris (*I'm OK—You're OK*) said, "Structure hunger is an outgrowth of recognition hunger which grew from the initial stroking hunger." [10] I learned to have specific tasks set up for the children whose actions cried out for the security of structure.

One morning I assigned partners, judiciously matched the night before, and asked them to follow the plan I had printed on the chalkboard.

1. Work on arithmetic for a half hour. Find out what your partner needs to work on and plan your time.

2. Read to each other from selections of your choice for a half hour. (A half hour was the minimal limit.)

3. Work on an art or science project for a half hour.

4. Free choice at the activity centers.

I had placed energetic, wisecracking Tim from a privileged home with restless, timorous Zed. Tim excelled in academic work; Zed was bright but had a learning disability and was embarrassed about his inability to tell time. My efforts to help him had been rebuffed. He protected himself with the premise that it is easier to take failure if you don't try too hard, then you can salve your ego by telling yourself that you could have done it if you had really wanted to. Tim was aware of Zed's defenses and tactfully offered to help him learn to tell time as his grandmother had taught him. Zed accepted the offer. (I shall never again underestimate peer power.) Before the morning was over, Zed was able to call out the time in hours and minutes!

Partner teaming paid off another time when volunteer third-graders came to our room to teach the children in Room 2 their newly acquired weaving skills. What a sight! Forty involved, concentrating children. Curly black heads and straight blond heads bent over a challenging task. Superior standard English background didn't count here. The poor reader who was skillful with his hands could teach the verbally gifted child and thereby gain a renewed sense of worth.

To break up room cliques and to provide leadership experiences while the children were learning about the responsibilities involved in self-direction, I selected heterogeneous groups of five for the organized learning center block. I made sure that the groups had the proper ethnic and sex ratios—no discrimination allowed. Each child in each group had an opportunity to be a leader. The rotating list was posted, and if the groups needed to be identified, we called them by the name of the current leader—no "crows" allowed. Even Kent's inner control improved dramatically on the days that he was a leader, though his authority never went unchallenged.

Our organized-center block of time usually followed a class meeting or a story in the early afternoon. Each group spent about thirty minutes at a given center. I was usually stationed at the math center, since I had to protect our borrowed Cuisenaire rods and other irreplaceable items. The problem of disappearing dice at the math center was solved after I announced: "I will not replace the dice *anymore*. No dice, no "dice games." The dice reappeared, and Reggie, an avid gamester, took it upon himself to be the guardian of the dice.

Moreover, I guided the children's explorations with the Cuisenaire rods. "How many pairs of numbers can you find that combine to make ten?" Children using the shape-sequenced, color-coded rods can investigate such problems even before they know number names. "Hey, teacher, I found out that the longer the rod is, the more pieces I can put together to make them match," Jay called out the first day he "messed around" with the rods. The joy was in the discovery.

We used our attendance charts and other kinds of personal information, such as the length of our feet, our height and weight, to develop graphs. We predicted, sorted, and classified whenever possible. I derived many useful ideas from the Nuffield mathematics series,[11] which consists of exciting idea books rather than work-books for children or teacher's manuals.

I'm not insinuating that we neglected the good old arithmetic facts. Drill cards were available, and the children often organized flash-card competitions during free-choice time. I learned that these children simply could not be pressured into learning facts or concepts. I could get them to parrot answers according to their ability to memorize, but is that learning?

The other four organized learning centers had to be self-sustaining. I made much use of cassette tapes. (The next time I open a classroom I will plan to spend weeks preparing learning tapes.) I could always anticipate trouble—sabotage of a neighbor's earphones or other disconcerting tricks—before the children would settle down to listen to tapes. I learned to stay out of the little conflicts unless it looked as if blood would be shed. The children settled down more quickly that way.

I placed various kinds of materials in the creative activities center, where the children could engage in paper sculpture, collage construction, and other art activities, as well as develop puppet shows (stick puppets were favorites) or write scripts for original dramas (only two or three attempted this). The art supervisor introduced a miniature version of cardboard carpentry in the form of hundreds of one-inch squares. When pasted edge to edge, the squares became edifices as unusual as the children's imagination and architectural talents could devise.

The reading center usually featured a machine, such as the Hoffman Reader [12] (lent by a friend), a fascinating combination of records, filmstrips, and work sheets that dispensed an amazing amount of information while developing reading skills. We also had individual filmstrip projectors available with filmstrips selected to correlate with a current project or unit of study.

There was less need for scheduling blocks of time for organized centers as the children became involved in constructive self-selected activities. This did not occur consistently until the last month of school—after the children had learned some group-relating skills.

I went to sleep evaluating the day's activities, often dreamed about the children, and had a recurring nightmare of being onstage in front of a large audience dressed in my slip. I interpreted that as my unconscious expressing a feeling of unpreparedness. Assuming that dreams do vent certain frustrations, I will credit them with helping me to wake up refreshed and ready to face each day with optimistic fervor. I tried to relax and have some fun on the weekends. One thing I could count on, attendance would be poor on Monday morning.

Successful Group Projects

Too many of the children did not have a relaxing fun time over the weekend. Tempers were usually short as the children straggled in on Monday morning. Many of the children lived in crowded conditions where "hit some-one and run" was the favorite pastime, and raw life was their daily diet. I wondered what I might do to start the week on a happier note (group singing didn't do the trick on Monday morning). Remembering the motivational power of the stomach, I broached the idea of turning our classroom into a bakery on Monday morning.

"What shall we bake next Monday?" I asked impulsively.

"Pie!" was the overwhelming response.

"Pie it shall be," I agreed, discarding any educationally sound motion of beginning with the simple and proceeding to the complex.

I spent the next Sunday afternoon gathering baking supplies and organizing materials so that twenty children (we had lost one) could be kept busy making cherry pies.

Monday morning: 100 percent attendance! The teacher in me couldn't let the golden moments of hushed anticipation pass without attempting some academic pursuits, so we started the day by copying the recipe for cherry pie.

"My momma already has a cherry pie recipe," Tricia

declared, hoping to get out of the copying assignment.

"Good," I replied, unmoved. "I don't think she has this one. When you finish copying the recipe, come up and get your baking supplies."

I had learned that it was pointless for me to invest energy in giving sequential directions to the entire group. I would instruct each child as he came to me for his cooking supplies. Eye-to-eye contact and a hand on the shoulder captured the attention of the most volatile mind, especially when cherry pie was to be the payoff. Furthermore the alert achievers prided themselves on listening in on the initial instructions and would proceed without further help. The ones I have dubbed "creative nonconformers" seemed to prefer eavesdropping while I repeated instructions to others. I saved effort and increased productivity by not attempting to instruct the entire group simultaneously.

The cherry pie experience should be written in psychedelic letters. The children were happily involved in a real-life, stomach-warming experience. Each child had created a pie complete with unique design pricked on the top crust. Graduates of a French pastry school couldn't have been prouder of their exotic creations than these children were of the trays of aromatic pies they carried through the halls from the oven in the boiler room.

Mouths were watering as the napkins and forks were handed out.

"Teacher, do we have to eat our pie?" questioned Reggie, who was always hungry.

"No. Don't you like cherry pie?" I counterqueried, frankly puzzled.

"Yeah, I love cherry pie"—said with smacking lips—

"but I want to take my pie home to my momma," Reggie answered, valiantly resisting temptation.

After that I had plenty of plastic wrapping on hand for our Monday bakery days. Inevitably the black children would wrap their goodies and take them home, sometimes yielding to a small nibble, whereas the white children feasted.

It seems redundant to list the incidental learnings that resulted from the baking sessions, yet they reinforce the efficacy of these methods. There was a productive discussion about yeast action when we baked bread. Again the children expressed their individualism by molding their dough into a variety of shapes although I had made no mention of anything but ordinary loaves.

Shaking cream into butter via baby-food jars seemed a miraculous yet feasible process to the children. Several of the children with gambling instincts laid wagers on how many minutes it would take to turn the cream into butter—mathematics with the "real spread." Individualism was again asserted when some aesthetic ones decided to use food coloring to create butter in various hues of the rainbow.

Colored in brilliant hues are the memories of the days when the children were involved in active pursuits that challenged their curiosity and satisfied their need to count for something. Some of the children were beginning to enjoy the challenge of paper work and asked for "lots of hard papers" to do. Those who were not capable of putting much down on paper were unperturbed by the prodigious achievements of those able to express themselves in this manner. Although I urged them to put forth maximum effort, they were well aware that their efforts would not be compared with someone else's efforts. Therefore some of the little wayfarers found renewed courage to keep trying.

One thing was certain, I was learning, and from all practical evidence the children were learning also. The projects I considered the most successful were those in which the children made choices. Each choice that succeeded was an affirmation of worth. There are no *failures* if instruction is truly personalized, because the options for success are never closed!

INVOLVEMENT OF PARENTS AND OTHERS

It has been my observation that teachers who learn to relax, relate, and rejoice with children will also relax, relate, and rejoice with parents.

The first day that Mrs. Love, a room mother, visited our classroom she assured me that the parents of the bused-in children would cooperate with me in every way. She informed me that four mothers and one father had been volunteering several hours a week as classroom aides, and Tim's grandfather spent all day Wednesday at the school. "Terrific. Their help will be invaluable," I enthused.

After the first week of having parents pop in at odd times during the school day my enthusiasm began to wane. The black children's reactions to the erratic measures of personal attention from the white parents seemed to swing from exaggerated feelings of self-importance to frustration at being the objects of such solicitous hovering.

I cannot deny that part of my dulled enthusiasm sprang from my own frustrations. For the first few weeks the cool-war power struggle was so intense, and the anxiety level so high, that the interruptions by the well-meaning parents and other visitors set off chain reactions of restlessness which could hardly be contained in a school setting. I was faced with a dilemma. I wanted an open classroom in the sense that parents and other visitors would feel free to come in and out at any time to join in the children's activities or just to observe. However, as long as their presence was upsetting to the children and to me, this relaxed openness would not be attained. (I would suggest that parent-teacher encounter groups be established at the beginning of the school year to hash out the essential ingredients of positive interaction and to establish guidelines for parental participation in the classroom.)

In Room 2 the children and the parents knew one another better than either group knew me, since they had had a semester's head start. These parents were aware of the hostility level and were distressed by the polarization. They had volunteered their children to demonstrate their concern for brotherhood and their belief in integration. Part of my anxiousness about their presence in the classroom came from my intense desire to be instrumental in solving the problems in the classroom and please everybody! The parents let me know that they expected great things from me, and I wasn't sure I could accomplish these wonders.

I held one evening parent meeting the first week. The room mothers phoned all the parents and offered them rides if necessary. All the white parents were represented, but only three black parents showed—J. B.'s mother and Marcia's parents. I briefly reviewed my philosophy of education and views on classroom control and management, and presented some innovations that I hoped to inaugurate. I outlined general plans for the year and suggested ways in which parents could help. We worked out a parent-aide schedule, and then chatted informally. How I wished more black parents had been there. I realized then that to establish the kind of rapport I wanted with these children, I should visit each black home. In the meantime I sent a class newsletter home with each child.

I fully appreciated the intent of the parent helpers but had to admit that their presence, under the circumstances, impeded my attempts to become a recognized group member. I became unduly annoyed when a socially prominent parent volunteer took two black boys out into the hall for a disciplinary lecture without mentioning it to me. I knew I would have to talk over expectations and responsibilities with each parent volunteer. One-to-one communciation can't be undersold. By trying to understand the basis for conflicting emotions and by keeping communciation channels open with parents, we were able to establish some positive and fruitful working relationships.

Peter's parents, the Loves, brought educational toys and games once a week. On that day for the hour before dismissal the children enjoyed the stimulation of new games and toys. Mrs. Love generally played with the children. She related well with them, and attention from an adult figure whom they could emulate was great for the children.

The children lost all school decorum when Peter's father dropped in. When this energetic, bearded father figure entered the room he was mobbed. Kent reacted to Mr. Love with more enthusiasm than he ever displayed around me or the children, and Butch and Torrance clung to his side.

Mr. Love was an ardent civil rights advocate, and I asked him to talk to the children on Martin Luther King, Jr.'s, birthday. Most of the children ignored his presentation, but they were pleased with a portrait of Mr. King which Mr. Love donated to the room. Kent had his picture taken while he reverently hung the portrait. When Mr. Love showed his slides to the children later in the year, Kent's self-esteem rose, like a barometer on a fair day, at the sight of his smiling likeness performing an important task.

The children loved Tim's grandfather, and Grandfather Smith loved the children. When he was in the room so many children were so intent on vying for his attention that they could concentrate on little else. Grandpa Smith was afraid he was impeding academic progress, so we agreed that he would relate to the group during recess and free-choice time and work with youngsters individually or in pairs for the rest of the day. He set up headquarters in the library and the children benefited greatly from the individual attention. The affinity the very old have for the very young is a delight to behold. If I ever teach a primary class again, I'll certainly round up at least one grandfather for the group to adopt. (I have heard of young children adopting patients in care homes—reading to them, bringing them goodies, and sharing class projects with them.) Grandfather Smith, though a rather typical

white Anglo-Saxon Protestant in many ways, had an un-
canny understanding of the black children's needs.

In fact, all the parents of the bused-in children showed
empathic understanding. They didn't draw color infer-
ences when their children reported a fight. They accepted
the subculture language patterns with equanimity and
were perceptive enough to appreciate the sociopsycho-
logical benefits of mixed ethnic groups. They were also
aware of the insidious effects of poverty. They did not
react negatively when the children didn't react positively
to their generous sharing. "Why'd you give me only one
candy bar?" "You always give me stuff last." "You never
try to help me." The parents were able to accept these
reactions without defensive retaliation because they had
some understanding of the poverty milieu. It is demeaning to be constantly on the receiving end of bountiful
gifts, knowing that one cannot return in kind. The children protected their pride and hung on to their identity
by feigning indifference and sometimes scorn.

I had to ferret out the black parents' cooperation by
visiting their homes. It takes time to woo and win, and
I just didn't have enough of it.

As an end-of-year celebration to honor the parents and
other friends, we decided to have a Pancake Fry. As the
children planned the festivity, *they* became the "do-
gooders" and got a taste of the blessedness of giving. I
urged the children to follow up their written invitations
with verbal supplications to their parents to be sure to
attend.

One day while the children were busy with prepara-
tions, I overheard the following conversation between
Zed and Butch:

"I asked my momma to come, but she say, 'Boy, don't bother me, I got other things to do,' " Zed mimicked.

"That's jus' what my momma say," Butch added, " 'Boy, you jus' quit takin' up my time. I ain't comin' to no school.' "

Butch noticed that I had overheard the conversation. His probing black eyes didn't miss my suppressed consternation. "Maybe my momma'd come if you'd come by our house and ask her," he said with gentle pleading. I couldn't help comparing this open, happy boy with the sullen, resentful child whose actions had impeded honest communication for so many weeks. We had developed an understanding that needed few words. "Will you stop by and ask my momma to come?" meant, "I believe in you."

What kind of curriculum objectives could predict outcomes like this? If Butch never learned to read, could his teacher be called a failure?

I stopped by Butch's house after school. His uncle opened the door and offered a surly, "What do you want?"

"I'm Mrs. Hershey, Butch's teacher," I answered, summoning courage as I smiled. "May I speak to Mrs. Brown?"

"Oh, you're Butch's teacher." The tone became friendlier. "Come on in."

Mrs. Brown, who had been declared mentally incompetent to raise her children without another full-time adult in the home, had bitter memories of her years spent in classes for the mentally handicapped. (I reveal my biases when I question the validity of the culturally biased tests that are used to label these children.)

Mrs. Brown's children were always sent to school

bathed and well fed. Butch was never absent from school with the excuse that he had to care for his little sister. Butch had absorbed a great deal of his mother's hostility toward "Whitey's System," but he had also absorbed loving care from home.

I had visited Mrs. Brown once before and had received nothing but grunted replies to my pleasantries, barely heard over the blaring television set. Her responses were more verbal this visit, but she expressed little interest in coming to school. I left her, saying, "Butch is counting big on your being there tomorrow."

"That's Butch's mamma," the children exclaimed, not hiding their surprise, as an impeccably dressed, but obviously nervous Mrs. Brown entered the room the following day. Butch did not hide his pride. After that, Mrs. Brown visited class one morning and went with us on a trip to Grandfather Smith's farm. "I wish I could have had chances to learn like that," she remarked when I took her home after our visit.

We had to make up a snow holiday on Good Friday, so the day called for a field trip. I remembered an incident that had happened after some troubled boys I had worked with were taken to visit a wild animal farm within driving distance of school. A tall, balding businessman who had given his Saturday for that excursion was well rewarded, and he often recounted his experience. "On the way home this kid reached over the front seat, put his arms around my neck and whispered in my ear, 'Mister, are you God?'"

I mentioned to our parent committee the idea of taking a field trip to this fascinating place and they immediately made the necessary arrangements. What a great self-image-building day it turned out to be. The children were allowed to pet many of the animals and to fondle the babies. Most of the children had to be restrained from getting too close to the "off limits" animals, but Julie and Kent hung back in terror.

When the children were taking turns riding llamas around a corral, Kent stood outside the fence fearfully hanging on to my hand. He had exhibited little warmth toward me in the past, but I became a secure refuge at a time when fear of the unfamiliar battled with natural curiosity and the drive for adventure. I searched for the right approach to help Kent overcome his fearful hesitation. Mr. Love provided the answer with a camera. "Kent, wouldn't you like to have your picture taken on the llama?" I didn't wait for an answer but pulled him through the gate and handed him to one of the friendly guides while giving the father a signal to take Kent's picture. Only Janie, who had surmounted her near-paralyzing fear of animals to attempt a llama ride, beamed as brightly as Kent did astride the gentle creature.

One project that involved parents and other interested community members was so successful that it deserves special mention. This was our Interest Club program. For this endeavor we enlisted the help of parents and other community members to conduct one-hour classes each Friday afternoon, along with teachers and staff members. All the recruited "teachers" could select a subject they especially enjoyed teaching, and the children could enroll in courses they especially enjoyed learning. All the classes in the school participated, using a K–3 and 4–6 division. This allowed for some healthy vertical regrouping and low teacher loads. Courses were offered in cooking, knitting, puppetry, creative dance, piano, horseback riding, lapidary, woodworking, and walking tours of local industry, among others. This project proved to be a joyful, satisfying learning experience for everyone involved. Along with happy children, one of the major beneficial outcomes was the enhanced spirit of cooperation between parents, community members, and teachers.

As the children and I began to take visitors and parent helpers in our stride, we welcomed the concerned attention and help these people gave as we struggled with the mechanics of learning.

A college physical-education instructor came by at least once a week. She would jump rope with the girls or organize a game with the boys at recess. She established a surprisingly warm relationship with Janie, and Debra adored her. She would jump up from whatever she was doing and call out for the world to hear, "Mrs. Wine's here!"

Since Mrs. Wine learned to know my children so well she became an invaluable sounding board for me. She would note improvement in attitudes and skills and comment about it. This was a bucket filler for me. Every teacher needs such a supporter.

I secured the tutorial help of several college students who needed field hours for an educational psychology class. I don't think that the aspiring teachers had learned enough about positive reinforcement; sometimes the children refused to go with the tutors even when they were promised a treat. I wondered if in their conscientious desire to teach something to these children, the tutors had given the impression that they valued the something more than the children?

One of the tutors was a locally prominent black basketball player. Thank goodness he impressed the white boys or he might have refused to come back to our room. "I don't ever want to play basketball, anyway," Kent said, unimpressed by the black giant's presence. "Football's my game," Torrance commented cockily. Butch refused to be the man's tutoree because he didn't want to reveal ignorance in front of him, so I placed a willing Jay with him, and temporarily shelved the idea of providing black male model figures for the black boys.

Overall I would evaluate the adult involvement in our classroom as a decidedly positive contribution. In one way or another the people who got involved with these children began to learn that there is an authoritarian way, a permissive way, and an effective way to work with them. The effective way involved democratic discipline that literally enforced itself because the rules became satisfactory to adult and child alike.[13] The parents and friends who became a part of the Room 2 experiment shared a vision of the laboratory of life that a school classroom could become.

CONCLUSIONS

Verily, brick by brick we built our "school-room." As the children came to believe that they were important human beings in a significant world, they chose to become involved in mixing "mortar" (meaningful activities), and laying "bricks" of honest understandings.

"Tricia and Marcia, don't you think it's time to go home? Your mothers will worry," I reminded them one day after school.

"We've got to get all these books straightened out first. We like *our* room to be neat," Tricia answered blithely.

I recalled the days when I couldn't force those two to straighten books in their own desks. Things had changed. I could leave small items such as felt pens and game trinkets lying around the room and they no longer disappeared. I remembered an incident involving Denver and a felt pen.

"Teacher, Denver stole your felt pen," tattled Jay, the watch bird. Accusing eyes focused on Denver; curious eyes shifted to me.

"I'll visit with Denver after school," I remarked with a reassuring smile. "Please get back to your activities."

No matter what disappeared, Denver was accused. It seemed that previous teachers had tried to "cleanse Denver's sticky fingers" by berating him in front of the children, and the children enjoyed his squirming humiliation. Denver had been cowed, but not cured.

During free-choice time that afternoon Denver furtively slipped the felt pen from his pocket to my desk. I nodded and smiled. (It is accepted.) After the children had gone and I was stuffing my briefcase with homework, I heard a rapping on the window. I looked up and there was a brown face, framed with cupped hands, wreathed in a grateful smile. I smiled back. (You are accepted.)

After that incident Denver made a great point of bringing me any felt pen or other tempting goody that might be lying around. I continued to hear reports of Denver's stealing outside our room, but the two of us had an unspoken pact. Room 2 belonged to the children. Why would they steal from themselves?

We changed things in Room 2. Not by superior pedagogical methods—most of them didn't work. We changed things by making mistakes and learning from them, by sharing our feelings honestly, by opening ourselves to the risks of close personal involvement. These were the identifiable steps to the way it was at last.

Part Three

The Way It Was at Last

Child
Curious

Seeing himself

Reflected in polished mirrors

Happy

Teacher
Finding herself

Accepted by those she would help

Rejoicing

Part Three

The Way It Was at Last

CREATIVITY AND OPENNESS

When the children in Room 2 began to utilize the materials at the activity centers to initiate their own research, create original puppet shows and other dramatic projections, make their own books, and eventually plan their own town, I knew we were on the road to meaningful open education.

The girls particularly enjoyed cutting, pasting, and finally, organizing and labeling. After they had finished several booklets on their volition, complete with descriptive sentences, I asked if they would like to read them to the kindergarten class. They did so with glee and were well received by the listeners. Four of the six girls began to instigate and follow through on many creative projects. Delightful (usually humorous) puppet shows, bulletin board displays, paper doll families complete with personalities and wardrobes, and homemade gifts for Mama were some of their accomplishments. Debra and Janie lacked self-direction and small muscle deftness. (The lack of deftness probably had a lot to do with the lack of discernible self-direction.) They often acted out their frustration by disturbing others, so I continued to give them directed activities, and whenever possible read with them while they snuggled close to me. One day Mrs. Wine tried to put her arm around Janie while she read to her. Janie promptly removed her arm and stated, "Only Mrs. Hershey can do that." (My "white witch" label was temporarily forgotten.) The "stroking hunger" was there, but so was the pride.

Some days all the children seemed content to spend hours in various corners of the room reading to one another. In four months four of these happy ones had advanced two years in reading according to a standardized reading inventory!

All but two of the boys reached the point where they were capable of constructive self-direction. Butch would "work," as he termed it, for a maximum of fifteen minutes, and then he would have to get up and move. Usually this meant trouble unless he could get involved in a checker game or sometimes Stratego or Monopoly. Checkers remained the favorite game for the boys. They didn't realize what an excellent math background they were getting, and the competitive scales weren't tipped in favor of previous school-oriented language experience. This was one arena where success was not determined by a standard English advantage. What a victory it was the day Butch beat Stan at checkers!

If allowing children to "play" during school time needs to be justified, maybe we could follow this line of reasoning: Children supposedly learn 63 percent of what they know from one another. If only about 10 percent of learning comes through our ears, and if learning by doing is

75 percent effective, it would follow that the most efficient route to learning would be to allow a great deal of peer involvement and interaction.

The all-important by-product of the game-playing was the emerging confidence I saw in the children. (Confidence is remembered success in something important to the child.) This confidence was displayed as the children became involved in new and novel approaches to solving old problems. (Creativity?)

A marked increase in acts of kindness, a rare commodity the first two months, was noteworthy proof of a definite swing toward feelings of self-worth. Zed and Reggie actually tried to talk through some of their differences instead of resorting to immediate fisticuffs. They had, heretofore, experienced failure in nearly every endeavor except those involving muscles. Both got "turned on" to checkers and experienced success outside the boxing arena. The patience and self-control they were learning through playing games transferred to other school activities.

I also saw Peter's unusual energies and natural leadership abilities channeled into creative productions. He became the acclaimed chairman of an underwater-life project. I had stored stacks of donated *National Geographic* magazines in the "hope chest" (hope someone would get turned on) area. Peter, Brad, and Butch were paging through the magazines one day and became excited about some pictures of underwater life. "That's what I want to be—a deep-sea diver!" Peter exclaimed. "Me too," Butch and Brad echoed. I tried to pick up on that kind of excitement, so I brought in a number of illustrated books on sea life and oceanography. Soon the boys emerged from the bus with armloads of books and objects related to the subject. A variety of shells were brought in, and Tim's mother showed us an unusual collection of mounted fish. Peter masterminded the creation of a huge mural depicting many forms of life in the deep. (I exulted in Peter's ingenuity and tactful leadership with his parents one day. We shared our feelings of joy over the revelation of children's energies transferred from subversive cool-war tactics to peaceful morale-building activities!)

Although I have admitted to racking my brain and calling on the gods of creativity for ideas that would promote productive thinking, the most pertinent and workable learning situations evolved from the children's self-chosen projects.

When some of the academic laggards discovered that learning to read and work with numbers could be a natural and happy experience, they began to structure many of their own learning experiences. One day a committee of children came to me with the request: "Could we have a town—and a mayor—and a judge—and policemen?" And so evolved Quietown U.S.A., pop. 20. I think they chose the name Quietown as a kind of lip service to my oft-repeated pleas for it to be "a little quieter in here, please."

The children elected a mayor, who selected council members to help her run the town, and a judge who settled complaints after recess. Sandy, an ebullient feminist, was elected mayor. She presided over the council meetings with an innate diplomacy. Peter was elected judge, a position coveted by Butch, who had been a natural adjudicator in our dramatic version of the children's favorite story, "Five Chinese Brothers." Sometimes when Butch came into the room in the morning "spoilin' for trouble," I gambled on his sense of humor and greeted him with, "Here come da judge!" It would usually bring a grin, and sometimes the good feeling lasted for a while.

Butch had a brief pouting spell when Peter was elected judge. He wondered if he had lost his standing with his brothers. He felt a little better when he was appointed chief of police, even though he had to take some ribbing and was called some barnyard names by Torrance. (He retaliated by deputizing Torrance.) The children taught me anew that our humanness is our common bond.

After several planning sessions the children worked diligently to set up a bank, a post office, a general store, a library, and a candy store. Then they invited first-graders to shop in their town. All proceeded smoothly until two store owners had an altercation, the origins of which I will never know. Suddenly the wares were rolling on the floor along with the owners. I decided that the constructive learning experiences had probably reached their zenith and closed the town to avoid a full-scale riot. Overall it was a very successful project with many unexpected learning outcomes. How dull it would be to revert to textbook parroting after such a stimulating simulation.

Three days before school was out we turned our room into a Pancake House. The children helped to rearrange the room, cut paper tablecloths, and fashioned crepe-paper decorations. This project sustained the interest of all the children. Tricia originated the design for crepe-paper flowers, Denver used his superior strength to push tables around, and Stan planned the program, while the other children were involved with menu-planning, writing invitations, and a myriad of other important details.

On the day of the Pancake Fry the children played their roles to the hilt. The hosts and hostesses performed with gracious dignity and needed little coaching to remind them to serve the guests first and to look out for others' needs before they served themselves. (For some this required superhuman self-control.) It was a soul-satisfying and appetite-pleasing experience.

Our brief program included poetry reading in honor of parents, directed by Stan, and group singing. The children chose some of their favorites: "Billie Boy," "Animal Fair," and "Kum Ba Yah," among others. They harmonized lustily while assuming informal positions in front of the room—lines were still resisted.

The principal was one of our honored guests, and after the event she sent us a large piece of newsprint with the message: "You are a great group. You had fun, and you are fun!"

SERENDIPITY II

My classroom was a microcosm of society's problems, but my faith in problem-solving through persistent dialogue has been confirmed. Indeed therein must lie the miracle. My belief in the essential goodness of human beings was strengthened. (Can hate survive when love is consistently offered?) I am not claiming that all the behavior patterns of the children changed dramatically, nor can I say that all outcomes were totally positive. I do know that although there were still some discordant notes in June, we were far more in tune than we were in January.

"Mrs. Hershey, why do you have hair on your arms like white folks?" Debra asked as she sat beside me in the car as we headed out for Grandpa Smith's farm the next to the last day of school. I can't recall my specific answer, but I do remember my feeling of joy as I thought: She's accepted me at last as one of her kind. It took some doing to translate my fair skin and blond hair, but however she did it we were now soul sisters.

As I drove to school on the last day, I told myself not to anticipate a grand and glorious finale, no matter how much I longed for a satisfying emotional climax to the tumultuous months. I had nostalgic twangs as I remembered last days of the past—special gifts, poetry in my honor, teary farewells. I reminded myself that these children had not conformed to any of my pat expectations, and our last day was sure to be another new experience. It was.

As the children entered the room, some of them dressed in their Sunday best, their faces revealed mixed emotions. Much like high and low pressure mixes, this could be a storm warning. I discarded any plans for reminiscing. The art supervisor, who knew of our penchant for checkers, had graciously provided us with materials for making checkers (bottoms of egg cartons) and construction paper checkerboards. This became our last day of school activity.

The children were happily engaged in weaving paper strips into checkerboards and transforming ecru rounds into red and white checkers, while the teacher was frantically busy supervising construction and mixing paint.

"Kent, pull your chair up closer to the table so you won't get paint on your pretty pants," I admonished.

My words of caution were characteristically ignored, and Kent's pants were soon decorated with red and black splatter designs. He couldn't bear the result of his clumsiness and had to find a scapegoat. He glanced at Peter, a good foot away, minding his own business, and declared sullenly, "Pete made me do it." Since it was the last day of school, I couldn't resist the Flip comment: "No, Kent, the debil made you do it." The smiles of the children, who had learned to tolerate Kent's outbursts, made me pause a moment in appreciation for the saving grace of humor.

When the final bell rang, I picked up the envelopes that held the atrocities called report cards. How could the interaction of the past few months be translated into the demeaning category of letter grades? I had included a personal letter to each parent in which I tried to give some meaningful appraisal of their child's progress and potential. The envelopes were sealed and addressed to the parents in an attempt to avert the inevitable comparison of the "unequal treatment of the *unequal*."

As I sorted the missives, the children pressed forward eager to be on their way. After all, the final bell had rung they seemed to say. About ten envelopes from completion, I heard a familiar wail, a stamping of feet, and choice words that were overridden by a judicial announcement from Butch: "Kent's gone crazy!"

I hurriedly finished handing out the envelopes, forgetting my dreams of fond farewells, and rushed back to Kent, expecting the worst. He appeared intact. Using my emergency tone of calm concern, I inquired about the problem. Looking down at a broken ringtoss spindle he had constructed in woodworking class, and pointing to a damaged checkerboard while clutching countless workbooks he had salvaged from wastebaskets, Kent sobbed, "I can't carry all this home."

"Kent," I chided, "haven't we always worked out our problems some way?" I helped him pack his possessions in a large paper sack. Wearing his glum expression, Kent left the room without bothering to answer.

"You can't win them all," I thought. But there was Stan's reply to my question during the final class meeting, "What did you like best about school this year?" "When you came to be our teacher," Stan had said, and he seldom expressed appreciation.

Then when a thoughtful Mrs. Love called to tell me that Peter was the only kid on the block who didn't want school to be out, I was warmed by the glow that accompanies successful effort.

My bucket ran over with tearful joy a few weeks after school was out when Dana brought me a candle apple and shyly expressed his appreciation for his teacher. Several days later I answered the telephone and heard someone ask timidly, "Do you know who this is?" I recognized the voice as one that had often been strident in expressing opposition to that "white witch." I also remembered some close, warm times with Janie. Evidently she remembered too.

"Is you gonna be my teacher next year?" she asked pleadingly.

"No, Janie," I replied, "but I wish I could be."

Please, whoever is Janie's teacher, look beyond the surface defiance and find the real Janie (Butch, Debra, Torrance)—and all the other young psyches that contain a bundle of hurts covered with scar tissue, daring some-one to love them as they are.

Teach these children gently. Be firm when you must. Don't feign affection; give it freely when you feel it. Great will be your reward in a small voice asking, "Is you gonna be my teacher?"

Notes

1. Bill Martin, Jr., *Sounds of Language Readers* (Holt, Rinehart & Winston, Inc., 1966).
2. William Glasser, M.D., *Schools Without Failure* (Harper & Row, Publishers, Inc., 1969), pp. 122–185.
3. Jerome S. Bruner, *The Process of Education* (Harvard University Press, 1961), p. 12.
4. Thomas A. Harris, *I'm OK—You're OK: A Practical Guide to Transactional Analysis* (Harper & Row, Publishers, Inc., 1969).
5. Dr. Donald O. Clifton, Lecture on Human Relations (630 Cottonwood Drive, Lincoln, Nebr.).
6. Ralph H. Ojemann and others, *A Teaching Program in Human Behavior and Mental Health* (Educational Research Council of America, 1960).
7. *Ibid.*, Handbook One.
8. Hugh Riordan, M.D., Consultant-President of Psyche, Inc. (434 N. Oliver, Wichita, Kans.).
9. George B. Leonard, *Education and Ecstasy* (Dell Publishing Company, Inc., 1968), p. 230.
10. Harris, *op. cit.*, p. 115.
11. Nuffield Foundation, Mathematics Project (John Wiley & Sons, Inc., 1967, 1968).
12. Hoffman Information System (5623 Peck Road, Arcadia, Calif.).
13. Thomas Gordon, *Parent Effectiveness Training* (Peter H. Wyden, Inc., 1970).

Resources

BOOKS

Arnspiger, V. Clyde, and James, Bill, *Values to Live By*. Steck-Vaughn Co., 1967.

Useful definitions and applications of values and their importance for all learning.

Aschner, Mary Jane, and Bish, Charles E. (eds.), *Productive Thinking in Education*. National Education Association, 1965.

A collection of papers by educators and psychologists outlining the productive and creative aspects in educating human beings.

Bruner, Jerome S., *The Process of Education*. Harvard University Press, 1961.

An explanation of the spiral curriculum theory.

Featherstone, Joseph, *Schools Where Children Learn*. Liveright Publishing Corporation, 1971.

A vivid description of the flexible, noncoercive British primary schools.

Furth, Hans G., *Piaget for Teachers*. Prentice-Hall, Inc., 1970.

Jean Piaget's monumental studies of the mental development of children interpreted for teachers.

Glasser, William, *Schools Without Failure*. Harper & Row, Publishers, Inc., 1969.

An application of reality therapy theories to contemporary education. Steps to involvement are clarified.

Gordon, Thomas, *Parent Effectiveness Training.* Peter H. Wyden, Inc., 1970.

Outlines the effective nonauthoritarian, nonpermissive way to rear responsible children.

Harris, Thomas A., *I'm OK—You're OK: A Practical Guide to Transactional Analysis.* Harper & Row, Publishers, Inc., 1969.

A readable interpretation of the parent-adult-child elements in human nature.

Herndon, James, *The Way It Spozed to Be.* Simon & Schuster, Inc., 1968.

A report on the classroom war behind the crisis in our schools.

Holt, John, *How Children Learn.* Pitman Publishing Corporation, 1967.

—— *How Children Fail.* Pitman Publishing Corporation, 1970.

Holt has a way of getting inside the minds of students and revealing what is going on there.

Howes, Virgil M. (ed.), *Individualization of Instruction: A Teaching Strategy; Individualizing Instruction in Reading and Social Studies; Individualizing Instruction in Science and Mathematics.* The Macmillan Company, 1970.

An invaluable series for teachers who want to understand and do.

Humphreys, Alice Lee, *Three Hear the Bells.* Funk & Wagnalls Company, Inc., 1963.

Poignant inspiration!

Kohl, Herbert, *The Open Classroom.* Random House, Inc., 1969.

A practical guide to a new way of organizing a classroom.

Leonard, George B., *Education and Ecstasy.* Dell Publishing Company, Inc., 1968.

An epochal book that celebrates the joy and the unity of learning and living.

Rosenthal, Robert, *Pygmalion in the Classroom.* Holt, Rinehart & Winston, Inc., 1968.

A graphic account of a self-fulfilling-prophecy experiment.

INSTRUCTIONAL MATERIALS

Creative Curriculum Guides

Nuffield Foundation, Mathematics Project, *Beginnings; Computation and Structure; Desk Calculators; I Do, and I Understand; Mathematics Begins; Pictorial Representation; Shape and Size.* Nuffield Mathematics Project materials for grades K-6, John Wiley & Sons, Inc., 1967, 1968.

Running through the work is the central notion that children must be set free to make their own discoveries and think for themselves, and so achieve understanding, instead of trying to learn through endless drills.

Ojemann, Ralph H., and others, *Materials from a Teaching Program in Human Behavior and Mental Health.* Educational Research Council of America, Rockefeller Building, Cleveland, Ohio.

Teacher's manuals, handbooks of pertinent stories, and other related materials designed to promote the causal approach to understanding human relations.

Ideas for Teaching Tools

Cudjoe, Freddie, and Ward, Johnnie, *Bulletin Board Ideas: Humanism in the Classroom.* Oklahoma City Public Schools, Oklahoma City, Okla.

Visual thought stimulators.

Darrow, Helen F., and Van Allen, R., *Independent Activities for Creative Learning.* Bureau of Publications, Teachers College Press, Columbia University, 1961.

For teachers who need help in getting children started on individual projects.

King, Pat Hopson, *Games That Teach.* International Center for Educational Development, Encino, Calif., 1971.

Illustrated collection of homemade teaching-game ideas.

Myers, R. E., and Torrance, E. Paul, *Invitations to Thinking and Doing et al.* Ginn & Company, 1965.

A series of handbooks with exercises designed to stimulate divergent thinking.

Tiedt, Sidney W. and Iris M., *Elementary Teacher's Complete Ideas Handbook.* Prentice-Hall, Inc., 1965.

Scores of teacher-tested techniques.

Manipulative Learning Materials

Cuisenaire Rods. Cuisenaire Company of America, Inc., 12 Church St., New Rochelle, N.Y.

Unit-scaled, color-coded rods that help children learn mathematics concepts through touch and sight.

Elementary Science Study, *Attribute Games and Problems Series.* McGraw-Hill Book Co., Inc., 1967, 1968.

Materials Related to Theories Discussed in Reality Therapy *and* Schools Without Failure

The Educator Training Center, 2140 S. Olympic Blvd., Los Angeles, Calif.

The ideas of relevance, thinking, and involvement are promoted through the media of books, tapes, and films.